THE WAY THROUGH THE WOODS

A CHILD'S ESCAPE THROUGH THE HAUNTED FORESTS OF WWII GERMANY

ANNA MARIA MANALO

PRAISE FOR THE WAY THROUGH THE WOODS

"Reminds me of the writing style of Elie Wiesel in 'Night' and 'The Hiding Place' by Corrie Ten Boom. A suspenseful and otherworldly tale rich with emotion and detail that will have you staying up late at night to find out what happens to the characters. The fact that it is based on true events makes it even more fascinating! Like all tales from WWII, it's also a great reminder to our modern society that absolute good and evil exist, we can't adopt the lie that morality is cultural or we will be doomed to repeat the atrocities of history. Highly recommended!"

- Nathan Harvey, Counselor and Author, Schwenksville, PA

"The struggles and hardships of traveling through the woods are told in such crisp heart-racing details that are so absorbing! I found this book very hard to put down as if I was caught in a runner's high and I just can't stop! The descriptions are so vivid that I was transported into the character and struggling as the character myself..."

- Jose Capuras, Retired IT executive, Cheshire, CT

"The twist at the end really got to me. Terrifying."

- Jenna Santiago, English Teacher, Riverside, CA.

"In league with writers like Kristen Hannah and Anthony Doerr's novel, 'All the Light We Cannot See', but it's an inspiring ghost story based on a real woman's life."

- Corrine Jo Meyer, Nonprofit Coordinator, Chicago, Il.

"Screenwriter-turned-novelist with a page-turner that left me awake until 3 a.m. I'll never go in the woods again."

- Walt Szczepaniak, Buckingham, PA.

" A remarkable story about a caring German family as they navigate the horrors of the rising Third Reich. The details of the settings and the emotions of the characters draw the reader into incredible experiences of the family. The courage and determination of these people make this true story one to be admired."

- Pamela B. Price, Retired teacher, Branford, CT

CONTENTS

They shut the road through the woods
    Seventy years ago.
    Weather and rain have undone it again
    And now you would never know
    There was once a road through the woods
    Before they planted the trees.
    It is under the coppice and heath,
    And the thin anemones.

- Rudyard Kipling, *"The Way Through the Woods"*

Published by: Beyond The Fray Publishing

ISBN 13: 978-1-954528-18-5

Beyond The Fray Publishing, a division of Beyond The Fray, LLC, San Diego, CA
www.beyondthefraypublishing.com

BEYOND THE FRAY
Publishing

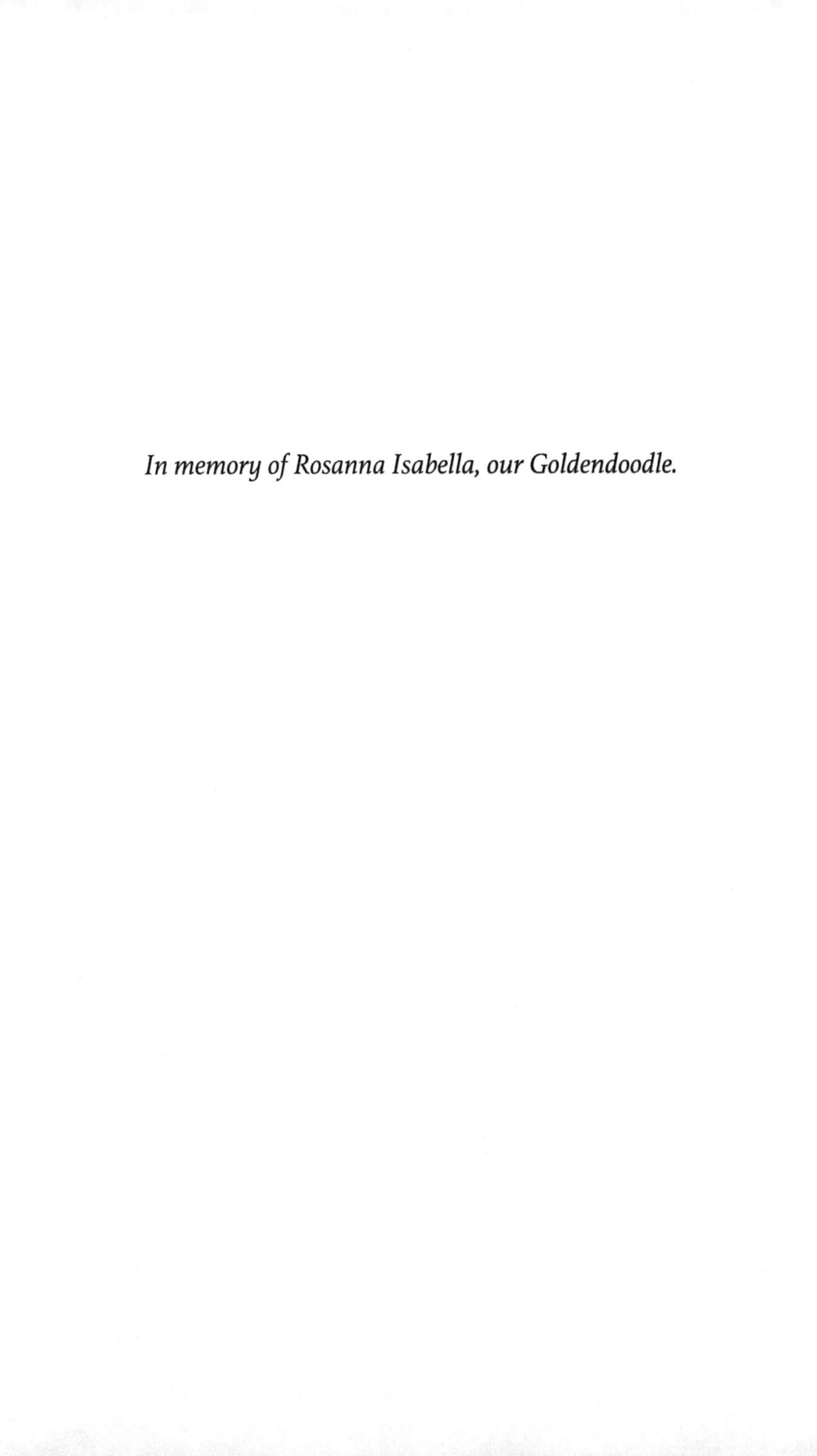

In memory of Rosanna Isabella, our Goldendoodle.

PREFACE

Bleichenbach sits approximately fifty-five kilometers northwest of Frankfurt, a village of no more than two hundred inhabitants, mostly a combination of modest stone and beam cottages. Today it has over eight hundred inhabitants. Surrounded by fields and forests, arable land and small agrarian farms for sheep, goats and vegetables, it was considered a prosperous, but humble village in the 1930s.

A couple, Horst Schneider and his wife, Agatha, settled in the village and soon had a daughter, Krista. Horst, slight and diminutive for a German, was raised as a child of pragmatic means, and he remained humble to a fault and well-meaning. His parents encouraged him to seek a trade he excelled in, and thus he became a tailor. Later on, this proved to determine the course of his life and the unexpected benevolence he received in the rapidly changing climate brewing in Berlin, which would cause millions of deaths.

Krista, age 6

While Horst worked in his shop in the center of the village, Agatha, also from humble means, the only child of weavers from northern Germany, embroidered handkerchiefs and shawls and tended to a vegetable garden. Krista helped her mother and played on the hearth floor as she listened to her sing.

This is their story and the terrifying events they witnessed when they entered the woods of Germany in order to flee.

In the natural world, animals only destroy each other

in order to feed and survive. Humans destroy out of greed, hate and intolerance. This book is about what happens outside the three-dimensional world when millions of humans are left without rights as human beings. This is when Mother Earth itself screams for justice. More importantly it is about the resiliency of spirit, the convergence of evil in the wilds of the forests – and the battle that ensues after the battle on the ground has destroyed all semblance of life.

I dedicate this book to those whose benevolence and compassion have overridden man's instinct to destroy. It is because of them, in both human, animal and spiritual form, that we have survivors of World War II. Krista is one of those survivors.

**This book is based on true events. Although the names of towns and villages given in this account are based on recollections of the heroine, names of individuals have been changed to protect them.*

Anna Maria Manalo
September 16, 2021
Buckingham, Pennsylvania

1

TODAY SOMETHING IS BREWING. Unlike other days, the horse cart passed under the bedroom window and stopped. Krista leans out in time to see her mother, Agatha, talking in animated whispers on the street below to a mustached man in his thirties, his shock of blond hair waffling in the wind. The bread man. By his side, a boy of eight, Josef, hands Agatha a fresh loaf of bread. Not the usual two, but one. Josef needs a haircut, Krista observes, his hair like his father's. Sensitive to the nuances of tone and body language even at her age of three, Krista notices her mom's undercurrent of anxiety in the staccato movements of her hands, her inflection and tone as she talks with the bread man.

Several miles away to the north, a man by the name of Adolf Hitler, previously an unknown artist, has just won recognition in the arena of politics. It is 1933.

Krista looks about, attempting to discern what has changed, her own blonde hair pinned severely in braids, two sides plaited like waffle-weave, the glow of the sun reflecting back. Krista wonders what created the change in her mother, but knows her mom will explain. She always comforts her and loves listening to her stories as Krista watches her embroider tablecloths, napkins and handkerchiefs. Always a patient child, she will wait. She pulls out a handkerchief with a pink peony embroidered on one corner and dabs her forehead with her small hands as she watches. Josef's eyes lock with hers, and he waves. Krista shyly waves back.

Krista's eyes wander above her and stop at the loudspeakers installed right under the roof of the last cottage where the village ends and the farm's fields begin. She traces the roof edges and notes that the speakers were installed, like large eyes, bowed down towards the narrow, cobbled street in groups of two every two houses.

She did not notice them before. *Why so many loudspeakers? Do we like music that much? One, two, one, two.* All the way to the Beckmanns'.

The Beckmanns are a family of four. They have a little girl her age, Mila. But Mila is different somehow. Her mom still brings her in a cart to visit, like a big baby. Mila is unsteady on her feet, unlike Krista, who was already running by age two and playing with the neighborhood cat and eyeing the neighborhood boys. Mila, her mother Emma said, was born that way. Her eyes are different than any other child in the village. They are swollen or smaller somehow, but she smiles and is always happy to see Krista. Mila makes everyone smile, including Krista, who is serious for her age and eagerly awaits going to morning school the following year.

Agatha takes Mila in once in a while to babysit as extra money in addition to her embroidery. Horst practices his tailoring skills and is successful in the village, but he has a touch and adeptness of style that also helps him to sell in far-off Frankfurt. Once in a while, they go there, and Krista marvels at the big buildings, the marble staircases and the shops full of clothes, ladies dressed and coiffed unlike her own mother – and the ice cream. The ice cream. It is like heaven on a cone. She likes trying them all – one scoop of raspberry, one scoop of espresso? *Yes, that's what it's called*, she thinks. Her father disapproves of a little girl eating coffee ice cream, but her mom allows it, as it is seldom. Those trips are rarely in their budget, so she allows her daughter these wonderful opportunities to savor what they couldn't otherwise obtain in their little village.

Krista recalls her father saying she would remain short like him if she drinks coffee at such a young age. When her fourth birthday came, Agatha treated her to coffee ice cream, and her father admonished her mother that the coffee would "stunt" her growth. "What does 'stunt' mean?" Krista asked. Horst said, "Stop growing tall." Mindful of her height, sometimes Krista would lick the cone, marveling and savoring every mouthful, secretly saying a prayer to baby Jesus, who sat with the Holy Mother on a table in their little entrance.

Today, they stay indoors, and Krista senses a change in the atmosphere there too. Then she notices her mother scurrying to the house where Mila lives. Instructed to peel the skin off the aubergines and shuck the corn while Agatha went to market, Krista perches herself on the wooden stool, reaching over the trestle table, rustic and pockmarked with age. She reaches for the large bowl of aubergines, a knife in her right hand, and gingerly starts peeling. She is very proud to do this, as it means her mother trusts her to do chores in the kitchen. She wasn't allowed that until this year. This year there were changes. Many of them. Today, another change, but other than the loud-speakers installed the year before, there is something else.

In her reverie, the knife slips, and she pierces her skin on one finger and bleeds. Brave and stoic, Krista drops the knife and sucks on the wound, staunching its flow. *Don't cry*, she thinks, even though it hurts. Her mother would never allow her back in the kitchen ever, ever again. *Don't cry. Be brave.*

Suddenly, a blast issues from the speakers from the window behind her.

"*Achtung! Achtung!*"

Krista forgets about her finger and steps off the stool, turning to the window, the smooth stone of the casement deep and welcoming. She clambers onto its thick surface warmed by the sun.

Outside, the bread man and a man and woman in a motor car, dressed in Sunday clothes, are staring up at the rooftop, paused like soldiers at attention. A few people, even two children, have stopped. She recognizes them from school and is in the act of calling out to them...

"*Herr Hitler. Deutschland steht am scheideweg zur grobe!*

In denkimmenden tagen wird es weitere ankundignungen geben!" (This is Herr Hitler. Germany is at a crossroads to greatness! There will be more announcements in the days to come!)

The children turn and wave at Krista.

"*Achtung! Sie mussen alle aufhören, wenn ankündigungen gemacht werden!*" (Attention! You are all to stop when the announcements are made!)

2

KRISTA TURNS from her peeling as Agatha enters, wrapped in a shawl, her dress dusty, hair disheveled. By her side, the stroller with Mila. The girl is smiling as if she just won the lottery.

"Close the shutters, Krista."

"What's the matter, Mama?"

"Please. Just shut them."

Krista steps up to the casement window and pulls the shutters together, turning the latch. In the dimmed kitchen, she examines her mother's face for the first time.

"Mama, who is that man in the loudspeaker who is angry? His voice is so loud and scary."

Her mother turns to the faucet, grabs a cloth, wets it, and wipes Mila's flushed face. Mila chortles.

"Hitler. And you will not speak of him."

"Who is Hitler?"

Agatha pauses. "It's better we not talk about him."

Krista watches her mother reach for Mila, taking her in

her arms. Mila's slight frame, much smaller than Krista, nestles comfortably in Agatha's slim arms.

"She's staying with us."

Krista squeals with delight. A playmate. She dashes across the room to Mila, but Agatha pulls the stroller away.

"I am putting her on the floor so you can play with her for now... but that's the last time here downstairs."

"Why, Mama?"

"Because you will say nothing about her being here. Do you understand?"

Krista, riveted to her mother's face, looks back in shock. Quickly, she surmises her mother's meaning. "She's hiding?"

Agatha nods. "Yes, but it's not a game. And if anyone finds out, including the landlady, we will all be in trouble."

"From the angry man? The one on the loudspeaker?"

Agatha nods again. "Yes. The man on the loudspeaker."

Agatha pulls Mila off the stroller and places her in the adjacent room, away from the front of the house.

Krista joins Mila on the floor of the adjacent room, shuts the window, and watches Mila play with a doll Agatha made for Krista.

"Where is Mila's mama?"

Agatha sits, a weight on her shoulders. Her sobs fill the room.

Krista stands and dashes to her mother's side to await her explanation.

3

Another week passes. One day, they hear the sound of marching. It is over the loudspeaker. Again sitting on the floor of the parlor, Mila points up towards the ceiling, unable to locate the source, cringing at the volume of it. Mila, so sensitive to nuances like Krista, shakes as if hit by an invisible force.

Agatha moves her low stool across the stone floor of the parlor towards Mila, in an attempt to comfort her as Krista continues to peer through the window slats of the shutters facing the street.

Agatha looks up from her knitting. "Is anyone coming?"

Krista continues to observe. "No one, Mama. Just regular people."

The loudspeaker booms. They jump.

"*Achtung! Achtung!*"

Suddenly, a knock on the door.

Agatha swiftly picks up Mila from the floor and dashes

two steps at a time up the wooden stairs. Krista makes for the door, but it opens too quickly.

On the threshold, hat in hand, is Horst, Krista's father. Krista visibly gives a giggle, a sigh of relief, and hugs his legs. Swiftly, he enters and shuts the door, bolting it again.

Upstairs, Agatha peers through the banister rails, pleasantly surprised, but Horst's face betrays an inward concern of what is happening outside.

The loudspeaker continues. Hitler's voice, reprimanding and intimidating, continues to announce his intentions in German. No one is listening.

Horst says, "We must talk."

Agatha gestures for him to come upstairs, and he removes his coat, hanging his hat in the foyer. He leans down and gives a kiss to Krista's forehead and takes her hand to go up the steps towards Agatha.

In Krista's small bedroom, they sit side by side, Krista by their feet, playing with Mila, who is sitting on a small blanket, surrounded by Krista's dolls.

Horst looks seriously at his wife, the weight of the conversation on him. "You know the Beckmanns were just escorted out of their house."

Agatha gives a look of shock.

Horst continues: "They gave them a week to deliver her to the police station. They didn't. They know someone's hiding her." He is looking down at Mila, who continues to play.

Krista looks up at her father's face, searching. "Why, Papa? Why are we hiding Mila?"

Agatha sighs. "How did the police know about Mila?

We hardly see them in the village. Mila is hardly out of the house except Sunday mass. Where did the Beckmanns go?!"

Horst looks down at his shoes, as if memorizing the leather creases. "People talk. Police and soldiers in town? They ask people. There are people eager to talk in exchange for..."

Agatha looks up. "For what? Where did they take them?"

"They took them to the train station."

"To go where?"

"I don't know. That's what Herr Beckmann asked. I overheard it from the landlady. He asked, and the soldiers said, 'Pack your things. You're all going to the train station to be relocated... unless you tell us where your daughter is.'"

"And?"

"She's here. With us."

Agatha stands. "But if I let her go..."

Horst nods solemnly. "Yes..."

Agatha motions for Krista to take Mila with her to her parents' bedroom. Krista obediently takes the girl and carries her, shutting the door behind her.

Agatha wrings her hands. "They will put her away, correct? Lock her up?"

Horst looks back in fright. "No, Agatha. Worse. They would kill her. Because she's disabled."

"Oh, my God, my God! So, they've been removed from our village and locked up instead until they surrender their own daughter!"

"Yes."

Agatha rapidly paces the floor. "I wondered what this was about. I wondered why they didn't want me to say anything. 'Just take her and hide her,' Emma said. 'Just take her, and I will come for her when it's over.'"

Krista reenters the room; her eyes go from one parent to another, searching, her body stiffening with every passing minute. "Papa, can Mila stay in my room? When will her mama return from the train station?"

Horst stands, preparing to leave. "I'm going to look into it. I am going to the train station."

Agatha looks back in fear. "NOW?!"

Outside, the loudspeaker has fallen silent. They missed the latest news.

Agatha pleads, "Please be careful! I didn't like Emma's tone. You know she's always very calm. I've never seen Emma Beckmann this way."

"I will bring them back here. Surely there must be some confusion. They are Germans like us."

Krista dashes to her mother's arms and hugs her.

The front door slams.

Mother and daughter look back at each other.

4

Horst resolutely strides through the market area, tipping his hat as passersby nod in greeting. He goes past the vendors, busy at this time of day. He crosses the only square in the village. He pauses to glance casually at his favorite shops, the tobacconist, the chocolates lining the windows of the local confectionery, and the pastry shop.

Horst makes a mental note to stop by the pastry shop on his way home from tailoring later that day, but the pressing matter of the Beckmann situation occupies him and pushes him on, resolute on a solution. Surely his respected status in the village will carry weight, and soon Mila will be reunited with her family. Or so he hopes.

He pauses at a corner of the street and sees the train station ahead. He sees a group huddled by the platform and searches for the Beckmanns. Emma and her husband, Gert, with their son, Hans, are standing together, holding each other in trepidation. A man in uniform wearing a white armband with a swastika smokes casually near them, a rifle at his side, his shoes all polished and glinting.

Horst crosses the street, approaching the train platform. Emma makes eye contact as Horst approaches, people staring at him, as his dress is impeccable, as his suit was tailored by no one else but himself.

Horst notices with perplexity that Emma is shaking her head vigorously, signaling not to interact. He pauses and realizes that this interlude may in fact cost Mila her life if he is not careful.

The soldier notices him and advances, blocking his way.

"*Zig Heil!*" The man clicks his polished boots together, raising his right arm stoically, palm forward.

Horst appears unimpressed.

"What is your business, sir?" The soldier's eyes glint, appraising Horst's tailored suit with envy.

"I'd like a word with you, if you please?"

"Certainly. Step this way, but not too far, as these people are under my care." The man gestures toward the group waiting nearby, including the Beckmanns.

"The Beckmanns here are my neighbors in this village. Is there a reason why they were asked to leave their home?"

The soldier clears his throat. He has a look of consternation.

"Herr... uh..."

"Herr Schneider."

"Of course. You're the tailor. Herr Schneider." He tips his hat with an eagle on it. He looks askance with distaste at the Beckmanns as both Emma and her son, Hans, watch. The meaning is not lost on Horst. Gert's face is almost beet red, the veins on his neck standing out. The soldier explains casually, "They have a daughter, you see... she is not like us and must be educated."

Horst raises an eyebrow. "Educated? A daughter?"

"Educated. Sent away. They won't let on where she is so that we can do our duty by her."

"Is that a valid reason to remove them from their home?"

The soldier looks away, discomfited. "I'm to follow instructions, sir, by order of the Fuhrer. They can return to their home once the child is located."

At this point Gert attempts to approach Horst, a look of terror on his face now betraying his red complexion. Horst lights a cigar, raising his hand for Gert to stop.

"You are sadly mistaken. I know them well. They have only one child. He's standing right there." He points to Hans, who smiles and approaches, clicking his heels in a salute.

"Yes, sir! I am soon to be a volunteer member of the Youth Corps!"

Confused, the soldier observes Hans, who in turn grins for the benefit of the charade. He is only ten years old, and the mandatory age for Hitler Youth Corps is twelve. The soldier looks on, impressed.

"I am the only child of the Beckmanns. Hans Beckmann at your service, sir!"

The soldier questioningly glances at another uniformed man nearby, who shrugs.

"At the service of the Reich am I!" Hans clicks his heels again and salutes with his right hand raised. "To the Fuhrer!"

The soldier pauses in thought, affected by the child's reply.

The soldier dashes to an army jeep nearby and places a call. A distinct chatter in rapid German ensues. He looks aghast by the end of the call. He puts the phone down and approaches the Beckmanns, including Horst in the conversation. The soldier appears very apologetic.

"I have advised my superior, Brigadefuhrer Stolz. He indicated that there was a woman in the village who is a Jew who has marked your family for some reason. You know of this Jew?"

The Beckmanns look on, now in a state of confusion and concern. To give the woman away meant death to her, but they know no one who would have talked. Yet. That saves them from lying and is salvation to their family. Horst looks away, musing.

"Who could be this woman? They have no enemies," Horst offers.

The soldier approaches the family, patting Hans on the head like a nice dog. "Please. On behalf of the Fuhrer, accept our apology. We have taken the message of a Jew against good Germans. You have our word this will not happen again. She will be severely reprimanded!"

With that, the soldier salutes again, Hans salutes, and the Beckmanns quickly step away from the platform and join Horst.

Horst, relieved but in a state of ambivalence, walks off quickly with the family and away from earshot.

Across the street in the safety of the square, they sit by the fountain, their voices muffled by the fountain and the passing carts laden with comestibles and sundries.

Emma asks, "What are we to do now?"

Gert replies, "We go back to the house and decide."

Horst says, "I suggest we keep Mila at my home for a few weeks and then see. Take it a week at a time."

Emma says, "But you will be in so much trouble... we can't put you in such..."

Horst says, "Nonsense. It's only until things calm down. A few weeks. Who is the Jewish woman they are talking about?"

The family looks at each other, searching their faces for a clue. They look back at Horst, clueless.

Horst looks at Hans. "We're proud of you."

Gert, the color on his face restored to normal, reaches for his son, hugging a shoulder. "A brave boy."

Emma approaches Horst thanking him and reaching for a hug. Horst reciprocates, glad to help their friends. Inwardly, he cringes at who might have given Mila away, and mentally goes through a list of Jewish friends.

5

Screams of women. Frantic voices. A forest comes into view. A set of bare feminine feet, wounded by the understory, attempt to walk. It is hot, humid, riven with the sound of cicadas. Men in uniform, soldiers with boots protecting their feet, trudge through thick undergrowth. Ahead of them, scores of women and men, young and old, are walking ahead with bare feet, some with slippers, like they were caught at leisure. Some are wearing dress shoes as if headed for Sunday mass or work.

A group of men and women are dragging a heavy wooden cart meant for horses to pull. It is laden with wooden barrels. The understory rips their feet as they wrestle for purchase, the bushes blocking the wooden wheels.

Among the walkers, one in particular has a cloth star hastily sewn and pinned to her breast. She has brown hair to her shoulders, matted and dirty. She appears to be in her forties. She is the owner of the wounded feet.

She falls, her eyes shut, pained. She cries. Irma, the Beckmanns' landlady. A soldier kicks her arm, urging her on with his rifle butt.

"Go on! Maybe you'll learn next time not to snitch on a good German family, bitch!"

He laughs as she gives him a stare, cold as the water ahead of them.

"But there won't be a next time, hey? Stop staring, or your eyes will come off."

She turns away, sobs as she gets on her feet, painfully trudging to join the others. She stops, ruminates an escape as the women trudge the waterline of the lake ahead.

"Go!"

The men and women amble into the water, grabbing pails and filling them. The exercise is pointless. They are collecting water for the garden to feed the army assembling in a week's time, they have been told. The army that will be garrisoned near their town. Why not just buy foodstuffs at the market?

An older man approaches one of the guards. He also has a lapel with a star on it. "Excuse me, sir, but the town has a sizable market with vegetables and meat. Why make a huge garden? It cannot be harvested in a week's time. Germination takes two months for some vegetables."

The guard stares back in consternation. "It's not for you to ask. You're not here to question the Fuhrer. Get to work."

Another woman approaches. "We need boots and proper attire. You can't just simply pull us from our regular jobs. We're not all farmers and..."

A rifle lands on her shoulder.

She gives a look of shock and pain as another woman screams.

Irma watches in terror. Her face wrinkles in fear, and she sobs. She grabs another bucketful of water and pours it into a large container on a cart.

Even though it's midsummer, Irma shivers.

The woman whose shoulder has been broken can no longer pick up her pail. As she struggles, a barefooted man tries to help her.

She turns to the man, eyes ever so grateful.

A shot rang out.

A thud.

She lies on the ground, a pool of blood forming around her neck.

6

KRISTA STANDS in front of the beveled mirror, slim, tall and beautiful in a blue gossamer dress. Her blonde hair glimmers against the morning sun from the open window, her shoulders slim, her demeanor graceful and feminine. She reaches for a perfume bottle nearby and spritzes some on her pulse.

Next to Krista, Mila, short and plump in comparison, smiles a broad smile with her freckled face and small eyes. Krista spritzes some of the perfume on her as well. Mila is wearing eye makeup to make her eyes look bigger, but it's mostly covered by bangs to hide it. She is wearing a pastel pink dress with yellow flowers, and she studies her reflection with Krista next to her.

Agatha does not like the dress. It makes Mila stand out too much for a girl who has grown accustomed to being in hiding. However, Krista insisted, as Mila can't go on living a life behind the walls of a home she has grown accustomed to, going back and forth at night to see her own parents under cover of darkness.

Krista and Mila approach the bedroom window and peer out.

It is Krista's twelfth birthday. In the side yard, they have two trestle tables laid out with food, cakes, and all manner of balloons for the occasion. Neighbors they recognize are milling about, fixing and tweaking flowers in vases, a dish here and there. Mila wants to stay inside despite the festive atmosphere, and Krista, now so close to the girl, like a sister she never had, has to reluctantly comply for the sake of her safety. However, there are no soldiers in sight, and for some reason things appear to have gotten better from season to season.

Outside, Agatha is busy entertaining, moving some of the dishes from the arriving neighbors to the appropriate table. Next to her, Emma Beckmann is fixing a flower arrangement, a spray of gladiolas and some lavender, which match the faded cloth tablecloth.

Agatha spots Irma Berman's younger sister, Sylvia, in a dull gray dress, wearing a cloth star pinned to her breast. She feels sorry for the young woman, barely twenty, who witnessed her sister being taken after she dutifully reported Mila to the census required by the Nazis.

Agatha feels guilt and remorse in her pallid frame for what she believes was a betrayal. The woman developed a tic right after the episode, and then a cloth star was shortly required of all the people of Jewish heritage in the village. The young woman baked a kugel, a sweet made from raisins, cinnamon and boiled noodles.

Agatha is so grateful the rent has not been raised as a way of keeping peace with her tenancy. Even when Horst approached the young woman, begging her to raise it, Sylvia fearfully refused, afraid she would also be betrayed like her sister. Agatha was saddened by the event, and Horst felt divided by his decision. Very divided.

Inside the house, Krista descends the stairs with Mila right behind her. Mila spots the large camera, a gift to Horst from a grateful client at the shop. She rushes to it, all coiffed in her new dress, and hands it to Krista, who props it on the table. It is so new she has to fiddle with the shutter. Horst spots them through the open window and rushes in, eager to begin the festivities.

"Please, try the new camera, Papa!"

Krista stands with one hand holding Mila's as Horst stands behind the large camera and aims.

"Say kisses!"

The girls giggle, and the shutter clicks.

Mila turns to Krista, giggling. "Will Josef be at the party?" She covers her mouth impishly.

Krista giggles back. "Who is Josef?!"

Mila laughs. "The bread man's son!"

"You like him?"

Mila laughs. She nods.

Krista covers her mouth, giggling. "I know your secret!"

Emma looks up and nudges Agatha as Krista exists like a grand young debutante, with Mila right behind her. Agatha hears Emma's breath catch in her throat as she quickly scans the other children nearby, who are eager and waiting to start the festivities. A group of women clap as a few men drink beer, raising their frosted glasses in Krista's direction.

No soldiers are in sight.

7

THE SCENTS of fine tobacco and leather permeate the shop. Horst stands with one foot on the raised dais, the man in front of him standing ramrod straight. The man appears impressive in his SS uniform, bearing the leaves on his lapel as a brigadefuhrer. Horst measures one leg and then moves to the other, noting with a pencil and pad the measurements. Around him, the leather sofas and paneling make for a well-appointed tailor's shop, the sconces bright and clean. It makes him proud to be part of this shop, which attests to his success and reputation as an accomplished tailor.

The customer clears his throat. "Do you always have it this busy?"

Horst looks up and pauses from his ministrations. "We do. All three of us have many customers, whom we feel fortunate to have, Herr Kommandant."

Brigadefuhrer Beyer continues to stand stoic, though a smile appears to play slowly on his face. He surveys the tailored clothing hanging from mannequins nearby, tastefully displayed. One other man is being measured by another tailor, and a third one enters the shop, to be greeted by a young man dressed in a well-tailored waistcoat. Both customers are also well-dressed in fashionable civilian clothing.

Horst wonders how the man he's measuring could afford the suit in time of war, but then notes the Nazi insignia on the man's outer coat nestled and primly folded on a nearby armchair. He shivers. Horst wonders what would happen should the man find some flaw in his tailoring. Crossing such a man would not be good for Horst, he decides. He is resolute that this is one client he needs to please among others. Probably more so for the sake of his family.

Horst steps away and gestures for the man to step down. He eyes the tea service on a nearby table. "May I interest you in some tea and biscuits before you leave, sir?"

The man clears his throat, putting on his jacket. Horst sees the SS pin on the man's lapel, the leaves on both collars. How did he even miss that?

"No, I must get going."

"Whatever pleases you, sir. Thank you for your patience."

"All good tailoring comes with patience, I'm sure."

"It does, sir."

"You appear to have an eye for detail."

"Thank you."

"And that meticulousness paid off."

"I'm glad it did, sir."

Horst dimly wonders where the conversation is going now that the man claimed to be in a hurry, but he has to go with the flow. The man has stepped down, and the other two tailors pause momentarily in their work to acknowledge his presence with a nod.

Horst thanks him again.

The man checks his watch, but strolls as if on inspection around the shop. He takes in the other clothes, pressed and hung on hooks, admiring, touching and grinning as he does.

Horst tries to explain the workmanship, but the man raises his hand to silence him.

A perceptible crack issues from Horst's knuckles.

He is perspiring and draws out a handkerchief.

The man folds his arms in front of himself. "Impeccable. These are your handiwork as well?"

"Yes. This part of the shop, sir."

The man eyes Horst. "How long?"

"Your suit, sir? In two weeks. I can arrange to have it delivered."

"Please don't trouble yourself. I will be happy to pick it up."

With that, the man strides away, stands by the door, and turns one hundred eighty degrees on his heel, snapping them together. "*Sig Heil!*"

Horst, unperturbed and prepared, salutes back with one arm forward.

The man walks out into the sunlight.

Horst looks down at his hand with curiosity.

The pencil has snapped in two.

8

THE FOREST BENDS to an unseen breeze, the silence broken only by few fluttering birds. The sun is close to its zenith and has begun to settle into a glaring heat. Despite the sunlight, a palpable loneliness descends on the forest. Towards the bottom of a hill, a group of bedraggled townspeople are dragging large logs on a pallet.

A large burning heap of logs can be seen in the distance. The group appears to be headed towards it, where other identical heaps also are piled and burning, giving off smoke like the others.

Coughing from several laboring people.

A large burning pile. Interspersed between the logs, a limb. It's mottled and pale and obviously human. Nearby, between logs, another limb, this one part of a leg. Attached is a pale foot, almost wooden in color, specked with mud and mottled as well. More nearby, burning and catching fire as the logs are consumed.

A few women are crying, dragging the logs at the same time. There are several piles in the clearing.

A man, old and frail in his seventies, falls. A soldier approaches, and the man raises his hands in a defensive posture.

A shot rings out, and the man falls flat.

Another woman cries, sobbing in agony.

Several yards away, obscured by a copse of trees and understory, Krista peers between leaves, watching in horror. She has just arrived with her little charges of children and walked away to take a discreet turn to relieve herself. She is wearing a dapper and pressed outfit of khaki and dark brown: A short-sleeve white shirt with a dark brown tie, a swastika pinning the tie against her chest, a skirt and long stockings to match. She is dressed as a Nazi Youth and so are the children.

Behind Krista, the children mill about, romping and playing as children do, drawing sketches on the ground with sticks they found. The oppressive heat of midday required a break, but the horrendous scene makes her gag. Krista turns her attention back to the children, some as young as four, some only a few years younger than her.

One child, a boy of about ten, approaches. Quickly, Krista blocks his view, wondering if he can hear the yelling from the soldiers, who are, in stern voices, ordering the miserable group of civilians.

Obviously, the boy can.

Krista tries to steer him away. "No, please. We're both too young to see..."

The boy gently pushes her hand away, his eyes exuding a look of puzzlement.

"Please. Don't make a sound," Krista admonishes.

The boy puts a finger to his lips, leans between two tree limbs, and watches in fascination. Krista is appalled at the boy's look, as his demeanor gives away a dreadful growing delight.

Enrapt at the scene of a group being approached by a soldier, Krista looks on in distaste and anxiety.

The soldier spits on a woman who is struggling to pull a cart with the help of three other women. The soldier is yelling obscenities in German.

The boy pantomimes the struggle of the women and laughs.

Krista pulls him away, a finger on her lips, a look of disapproval on her face.

The boy leaps to the ground as the soldier turns, hearing him.

The soldier raises his rifle, surveying the wood.

Krista whispers, "Don't."

She leans behind the tree, trying to disappear.

The boy sneers back in defiance. "I don't care. He can come here, and we can say we just wanted to learn tactics."

Krista reels back in consternation.

The boy's bravado bothers Krista. What she is doing is teaching these kids that it is all right to hurt others because they are different. It is so against what her parents believe in.

With growing horror Krista realizes that this boy could grow to become a "brownshirt" – a civilian who snitches on others on behalf of the Reich. They are called brownshirts because they wear a brown drab uniform from head to toe, identifying them as the eyes and ears of the Nazis. They assist the Reich like demons assist Satan. What if this boy finds out that Agatha is hiding a disabled girl? As his teacher, would this boy betray her at the cost of her mother and Mila?

The soldier lowers his rifle and turns away, losing interest. He turns back to watching his group pulling the heavily laden cart full of logs. A woman appears like she is about to have a heart attack. Her face, sweaty, red and bulging with effort, makes Krista's own heart burst with anger and injustice. That woman could easily be her own mother. She watches the boy next to her stand, wipe soil off his short pants, and rejoin the group in the meadow. It was as if he were just watching a soccer match.

Krista shivers even though it is hot, realizing this boy would be as ruthless as the soldiers.

Reluctantly, Krista rejoins her young charges, about twelve in all, hazarding a glance back at the trees that shield her and her group from the demented violence several yards away.

The boy approaches the group and eagerly tells them what he saw.

A few of the students gasp in horror. They look at Krista for an explanation.

Krista, unable to provide a quick explanation, gestures impatiently for them to keep going. A little girl of four approaches and reaches for her hand as they walk, and another girl hangs onto Krista's starched skirt, seeking solace.

"Everyone, go quickly now, as lunch is waiting for us. The last one will not get lunch."

The two little girls dash away, following the group.

The rest romp ahead without a care in the world as she follows behind, grabbing her books from the grass, the Nazi swastika plain on the binding of the book in her hands.

Krista walks, watching her charges, touching the head of the four-year-old with affection as she passes. She frowns, wondering what will happen to them.

9

KRISTA AWAKENS IN A DARK WOOD, the face of a bloody woman in tatters hovering a few inches from her face. The woman's hair is matted with soil, snails clinging to her filthy locks. The snails fall on Krista, clinging to her face, her clothes, her hair. She vainly tries to brush them off with her hands, but she's unable to move.

One large snail crawls inches away from her eyes.

She can't find her voice.

Finally, she screams.

Sunlight. The door to her bedroom swings open.

Krista awakens in bed as Agatha approaches in alarm.

"You were having a nightmare."

Agatha sits by her side as Krista sits up and reaches for her mother. Mila stands at the doorway in pajamas, looking on with a look of concern.

"It's early, but your father has left for the shop."

"Sorry to scare you, Mama. A bad dream."

"Come and have breakfast. You'll feel better."

Mila waves Krista a wave of "Come and join us."

Agatha ushers Mila back to the kitchen. "Come, let her get washed and dressed. We're going to see your mama tonight."

Mila smiles a wide smile, clapping her hands in silence.

Krista watches them leave as she descends from her bed, a look of worry and love on her face.

In the kitchen, Agatha pours Mila a glass of lemonade from a frosted green pitcher filled with lemon slices. She sees Mila's reflection through the pitcher as the teen consumes one small pancake after another.

Mila gained some weight in early adolescence, and it had become more difficult for Agatha to explain what the bolts of flowered cloth were for that she gave to Horst in his tailor shop. "Why so big a cut?" one woman said at the fabric store. Was Agatha pregnant? Agatha hated the questions and had to explain that it was a new style her husband was trying, as he also made clothing for women. "He's a trendsetter," Agatha confided. Then the woman indicated she wanted to see it on her when it was finished.

Later that day, Agatha told Emma she would need her to purchase her own cloth, as the fabrics were arousing suspicion with the seller. Emma decided with Agatha that she would need to be more prudent in purchasing solid colors instead of flowers to explain away that they were for her husband and son instead of a daughter who wasn't supposed to exist. If only their village weren't so nosy.

A few weeks later, Agatha went with Horst to Frankfurt, taking Emma along to shop in the large fabric stores where no one knew them, as it was a city where those questions were no longer asked.

Krista walks down the steps, one at a time, her dress the worse for wear. It is a Saturday morning, she recalls, and it is her father's turn to mind the shop on a weekend. Today, like other Saturdays when her father is working, is a day of washing and hanging clothes, pulling weeds from their small vegetable garden, and playing in the twilight before dinner. There's no point in wearing her good clothing, as there is no school.

Then she remembers with a feeling akin to dread that now during the week she is a Youth Corps teacher and has to wear the dull khaki uniform issued by the heavy lady. What was that woman's name again? The buxom woman spoke to her parents a month ago, dropping off books for Krista to use in indoctrinating the "charges" assigned to her. In one of the books she is supposed to study, a list of things to remember made Krista inwardly cringe.

Do Teach: The Aryan race is under threat.

Do Teach: Blonde hair and blue eyes are a sign of the pure Aryan race.

Do Teach: Report all NON-Aryans.

Do Teach: It is our duty as citizens to report all Jews, children with racial deformities and blood impurities.

Krista was taken aback, reading and rereading what the book said. *What is a racial deformity? What's "blood impurity"*? She turned the pages, and there picture after picture of children who were offspring of women who were from other countries: Asian, Black, and some with different hair texture and eyes not as wide or blue as hers.

Then one page showed children they called "Retarded" or "Mongoloid." Krista was fascinated, but then repulsed. *Why rid the world of them? Aren't we as citizens supposed to help them because they are at a disadvantage?*

It kept going:

Do Teach: Good German citizens must be loyal and salute whenever possible. Teach proper salute.

And so on and so on.

Krista yawned at the monotonous list of do's and don'ts. Don't argue, don't ask, don't be dirty. Racially impure people are dirty.

Krista sat back, thinking of her history and geography books where people ate, dressed and practiced customs and traditions that were different from her village. She thought they were interesting and wanted to visit those places when she grew up. These people were racially different.

In the kitchen, Krista sits across from Mila and Agatha, who nudges a bowl of oatmeal towards her, dotted with almond slivers and golden raisins. Mila instantly frowns, taking in Krista's somber mood. "Krista, why are you sad?"

"Not sad. Just thinking about my nightmare."

Mila pouts. "I didn't do anything wrong, did I?"

Agatha notices and turns to Mila. "Mila, your bath is waiting for you. Why don't you go ahead while Krista eats, and let me clean up breakfast?"

Mila gives Krista a quick kiss on the cheek before she steps off the stool and climbs the stairs.

Agatha watches Mila climb up the steps and disappear into the upstairs bathroom. She glances back at Krista, who looks forlorn and very concerned. She stands and opens the kitchen window to the breeze of early morning. It has a view of the quiet street. Agatha returns to her stool, joining Krista at the table.

"What happened yesterday? You haven't been the same since you came home from teaching."

Krista plays with her oatmeal, trying not to add to the growing burdens in the household. She takes a spoonful of the hot porridge, but doesn't reply.

"I'm listening, Krista. I am here for you."

Krista takes another spoonful of the oatmeal and finally replies, "Mama, do you know what the books are about that the lady gave me to teach the children?"

Agatha gives back a look of trepidation. "No. I wish your father and I had a chance to look through them. What are they about?"

Krista's eyes well with tears. "When I first got them? I had to look through them and read the first one... then I had to study them? So, I did."

"And?"

"I will show you. Some are about Mila's type of person..."

Agatha wipes at the tablecloth, deep in thought.

"Mama?"

Agatha looks at the view outside the kitchen window from where they sit. The birds are chirping. It is a lovely day.

"Mila is being called retarded. Mongoloid?"

Agatha solemnly nods.

Krista observes. "Is she?"

"Now you know how dangerous it is for us."

"How could they?!"

Agatha reaches for her daughter's hand, the spoon now resting on the napkin, the oatmeal partially eaten. The hand she holds is cold, clammy.

"Mama, yesterday there was a meadow where I took the children to rest."

"Yes?"

"It was around lunchtime. I wasn't expecting to see anyone... but there were soldiers and prisoners in that part of the woods. I don't know if they were prisoners, but the soldiers were forcing this group of people to work... they were so cruel to them..." Krista goes on to tell Agatha what she saw and the boy's reaction, which troubled her.

"What you saw was forced labor. Most are probably Jews from around here or from as far as Poland."

Krista starts crying. "Do I have to keep teaching what it says, Mama? Do I?"

Agatha stands, comes around the table, and takes her daughter in her arms. "I'm so sorry you had to see that. So sorry!"

Krista looks up at her mother, a look of horror in her eyes. "What is to become of you if they catch you with Mila?"

"Krista! The window is open!"

For several years now, it was the elephant in the room, which was left unspoken. Krista brought it to the light of day.

Agatha shakes her head. "I don't know. I pray we don't have to get to that, my dearest."

"You have to think it through, Mama. You have to see what they're doing to them."

"I know. I know."

Agatha pulls up a stool, draws her daughter to her, and they rock together, crying.

"Mama, I love Mila, but if we are caught with her..."

On the top of the stairs, Mila sits watching and listening. She takes it all in and appears to understand.

10

STRAINING to lean out of the deep recess of the windowsill, Mila finally climbs on it and sits. She follows the cobbled path of the street below with her eyes. Finally, her eyes rest where the slim figure of Agatha is walking, receding in the distance of the street, deserted and misty early in the morning. She notes the street signs. Agatha told them earlier that day she is going to market to sell her embroidery and then coming back by noon for lunch.

Mila recalls the market. There is a train station nearby.

On paper from her pocket, she draws a sketch of the streets with her little fingers, using a pencil. Then she steps down into the bedroom, a simple room decorated with yellow flowers on the walls. Yellow is her favorite color.

On a small bed with an iron headboard, Mila has an open suitcase filled with her clothes, some which need mending, some new. She presses a small notebook into a corner, then pauses. Changing her mind, she picks up the notebook and opens it. A photo of Josef, the bread man's son, falls out. She slips it back in and pockets the notebook. She looks up towards the door, where her straw hat hangs on a hook, and pauses. Tears well in her eyes. Mila quickly wipes away the tears with her sleeves and looks up at the clock on the wall. It is close to 7 a.m.

Down below, she hears Krista's footsteps trudge up the wooden stairs. Quickly she shuts the suitcase and pushes it underneath the narrow bed. She smooths the newly made bed, practiced from years of pretending it is a spare bedroom, as it is supposed to be. Empty, untenanted and lonely for a guest.

A knock on the door.

"Come in."

Krista peers in, a grin on her face. "Got time to help me pull weeds from the garden?"

Mila steps away from the bed, wipes her hands on her threadbare dress, and nods with zeal.

Too eager, Krista thinks. *Pulling weeds is not one of Mila's favorite chores. Maybe she's eager to get out of the house.*

The vegetable garden is sizable, in varying stages of growth. Cabbages, rutabagas, and turnips, newly harvested, lay in a heap near a row of spinach and tomatoes. A row of trees on one side obscures them from the field beyond, a small hill from the back.

A small pail with gardening tools stands nearby. Krista grabs it as Mila hunches over a low patch of weedy ground between rows of broccoli. Krista hands Mila a trowel to help dig up the weeds, and she takes a row a few feet from her. Krista's back turns as she hunches down to start the arduous but necessary task.

Krista starts humming a tune to pass the time and then breaks into a song. It is a tune her father used to play on the piano when she was young.

Mila joins in the refrain: "*Schon ist die nacht...*"

Krista sings, turning to glance at Mila, who has a pretty voice, though a bit out of tune. She continues singing. It helps to pass the time and makes the chore more enjoyable.

A rabbit emerges from its burrow nearby, and Krista pauses from her work to observe it, still humming the tune. Lost in thought, Krista watches the rabbit hop around the turnips, sniffing them with its pink nose.

The sun is emerging behind the clouds. Krista pulls out a handkerchief with a pink peony embroidered on one corner. She dabs her forehead with it.

The rabbit hops away. She turns to see if Mila saw it.

Mila is gone.

Krista stands, wiping the sweat from her forehead. She decides to follow Mila into the house, eager for a cool drink.

She walks into the kitchen, but Mila isn't there.

She pours a cool pitcher of lemonade from the morning's breakfast and pulls another glass from the cabinet.

Silence.

"Mila!"

She pours the second glass of lemonade.

"Mila."

She walks into the small parlor. No Mila.

Upstairs, in Mila's bedroom, Krista pushes the small table, where a washbowl sits, away from the wall where a closet is hidden. Krista gets down on her hands and knees and pushes the door open, revealing the dusty entrance to the attic.

"Mila? Did something scare you?"

11

AGATHA SHOULDERS her way past the throngs of women looking at baskets and all manner of leather goods. A heavyset woman accidentally pushes too close, almost upending Agatha's basket of goods. Agatha pauses to check the eggs and meat that lay parceled among the bread. A good sale of embroidered handkerchiefs yielded good food and much-needed bread. The bread man had stopped coming, now recruited to help build shells for the army.

Between people milling about, she spots, to her consternation, Mila walking with a piece of luggage, trudging breathless among the sellers and customers.

Agatha takes a second look in disbelief. "Mila?"

At a loss as to what to do, Agatha follows, unsure if she is seeing Mila or someone who resembles her. Until she recognizes the dress that she just mended a few days before.

It is Mila. She can't yell her name. All she can do is

follow her and try to catch her undetected amongst the throng of customers. Mila appears lost and searching. The girl appears to be headed for the square, an open area.

"Oh no."

Agatha dashes after the girl, now unheeding the peril. Two German soldiers stand by the edge of the square, chatting, smoking. Mila passes them, but they do not see her. Above Agatha, a Nazi flag waves in the air, suspended from a building.

A boy of ten approaches Mila, grabbing her suitcase. "Train to catch?"

It is the boy who was watching the group of civilians with Krista the day before. The one who took delight in what the soldiers were doing to the civilians as they labored.

Mila half-smiles, unsure. "Yes?"

"I can carry it for you."

The boy walks confidently as if the suitcase isn't heavy. Mila follows, relieved she doesn't have to carry it. On the back of the boy's collar, a khaki outfit with a white shirt, Mila sees an embroidered swastika. It looks familiar.

Then she remembers what it means. It is the same uniform Krista wears during school days.

Then she frowns, recalling the conversation she overheard at breakfast.

Mila, seized suddenly with fear, tries to grab her suitcase. "I can take it now."

The boy ignores her, a grin on his face. "It's not a problem."

Mila dashes up to the boy and grabs it.

He lets it go. "All right, snake eyes. If you insist."

He walks off.

Agatha watches the interlude and sighs in relief when the boy walks away. Then she follows him with her eyes, her basket clutched in her hands, knuckles tense and white.

He approaches the two soldiers who were smoking and points out Mila, who is walking with determination to the train platform.

Agatha dashes to the side and stops, unable to breathe. She is torn, unable to decide whether to save Mila or to save her family.

Under her breath, she whispers, "I'm sorry, Emma!"

She turns to walk away and then hears a whistle. Quickly she walks toward the side street, past several sellers, trying to avoid detection. Guilt and something like agony assail her features as she turns to watch from behind a row of crated vegetables at a stand.

On the boy's tip, the soldiers have taken Mila's luggage as the taller one pulls her by the hand. Mila appears to be questioning the man, who is smiling down at her. Finally, she relents. He has convinced her to go with him.

Agatha emerges from behind the stall of vegetable crates and follows from a distance. The soldier stops and tosses the luggage into the back of a cart. Then they both pick up Mila and push her into the back of a black truck. Several people appear to be lined on the pavement, waiting to enter. Mila was the first to enter.

Then Mila reappears, squeezing herself through a front window, and drops to the ground.

A soldier quickly turns and grabs Mila, hauling her back to the truck. Mila appears angry.

The rest of the people are now being forced with rifles to enter the truck. There is commotion, yelling, mayhem.

Agatha sways in shock.

She drops her basket, rooted to the ground.

She picks it up, tears welling.

Between the tears, she sees her eggs in the basket have all broken, but one.

12

Horst efficiently brushes the new Nazi uniform, the lapel glinting with the insignia of the SS. Around him, handsomely tailored men's clothing hangs, covering the walls in style like a department store in Paris. Hats of all sorts complement the shelves. Here and there women's clothing of the day fashionably displayed on mannequins with matching shoes and hats.

The door opens, and the man Brigadefuhrer Beyer, who ordered the suit from two weeks ago, enters, salutes Nazi style, and Horst salutes back without resolve. He is still tentative, but willing himself to please and to remain obscure for the sake of his family.

The man, tall and slim, a commanding figure among the few customers that bright afternoon, smiles when he sees the uniform Horst made for him. He touches it as if in worship, walks around it, and pauses. Horst has the new outfit displayed on a hanger by itself, the pants hanging and shoes to match also displayed on a pedestal reserved for customers to admire.

The man looks down at Horst, a few inches taller than he. "Perfectly styled. You do elegant work."

"Thank you, Herr Kommandant."

Horst offers the nearby tea service, a set of fine bone china in hues of pastel green and light pink. The service is markedly more feminine than Horst and his colleagues would have liked, but Agatha picked it out, as it was a fashionable "lusterware". The pot is still steaming. Tastefully decorated with teacups to match by Ostermark of Bavaria, it glints in the light of the sconces and chandelier.

The man eyes the confections instead, unimpressed by the tea. He grabs one quickly from a cake plate gilded in gold and pops it in his mouth.

"Again, I need to pass on the tea. Perhaps next time."

"Yes, perhaps in the future."

The man muses, looking away. "I'd like to please ask you a favor."

Horst raises an eyebrow. "Yes?"

"I have a few friends here... they need tailoring as well. In the same style, you see."

Horst nods, glad to get more customers.

The man eyes him with meaning. "For the men. In service of the Reich."

Horst attempts to glean whether the man is asking him to make the uniforms for free.

The man quickly sums up Horst's look. "For a very handsome fee of course."

Horst inwardly relaxes. Food and rent were raised

recently, and the vegetable garden is only yielding a harvest barely fit for the family. *Mila eats a lot*, he thinks. He is thinking he can really use the account, as Agatha is at the market, getting eggs and meat, which are getting more and more expensive. It appears that most of it is being reserved for the German soldiers and their elite, who do not purchase handkerchiefs or dainty towels for their wives.

"Of course. I will be happy to see them. But the material for this garment..." Horst is thinking how more and more the fabrics are also getting hard to procure.

"That won't be a problem. The Reich will provide it for you, and only your labor is needed. Er... I mean your expertise. Your tailoring, which is impeccable."

Horst feels himself blush at the compliment, wondering what is next.

"You live nearby?"

"Yes. Bleichenbach, Herr Kommandant."

The man pauses, taking in the furniture of the shop, which is high-end, polished wood. Beech. "Why not Frankfurt?"

Horst has to think.

"Too far from the shop?"

"Yes, Herr... we like the small village atmosphere too."

The man is deep in thought. "The Schneiders of Bleichenbach. I seem to recall a few rental homes there..."

Horst nods, now tentative. He recalls the incident where he had to intervene for the Beckmanns.

"You are renting... or were renting from a Jewish woman, correct?"

"Her sister, yes." Horst is now distraught, wondering if this confession will lead to difficulties.

The man clears his throat. "You need a proper house. You need not rent, especially from a heathen."

Horst is sweating now. "The rent has not been raised for several years, until recently, and we are grateful for the past kindness. Times are hard, Herr Kommandant."

"I understand, but for a man of your caliber, it should never be raised." This is said in a tone of reproach.

Without hesitation, the man takes the clothing from the hanger and strides to the door. He turns as Horst salutes in a fashion that clearly is out of duty to protect his family. The man salutes back.

"Herr Schneider, from this day forward, your lodging is free. I will see to it that you are properly accommodated."

The man turns, strides out. A chauffeur, manicured and dressed in a uniform for a livery, opens the passenger back door to let the kommandant in.

Horst shuts his eyes, but it isn't against the sun's glare from the gleaming car outside.

13

AGATHA DEJECTEDLY DROPS the basket by the front door, entering, crying. Krista dashes to her mother as Agatha shuts the door behind her.

"Mama, I cannot find..."

"Mila. Yes, she has been caught!"

Krista looks back, aghast.

Agatha enters, looking defeated. "She must have overheard our conversation this morning."

"Oh, Mama! How could she?!"

"She did and had a suitcase with her."

"Where is she now?!"

Agatha looks out the window. Down to the right, a few doors down, at the edge of the street, is the Beckmanns'. "Stay here, Krista. If you hear or see anyone in uniform, run upstairs and hide where Mila used to go."

"Why, Mama?"

Agatha looks back in terror. "Because, my dear, if they

find out from her how she evaded being detected, we are done!"

Krista's face is a mirror of growing dread. "You don't think they would..."

Agatha nods. "They just might. I have to go tell Emma. I have to tell her what happened. Prepare her for the worst and make sure she knows they're in peril now."

"Wait, Mama. What if the soldiers are coming! They can't see you!"

Agatha breaks away, shaking her head. "I have to tell Emma. At least she should know her daughter is gone."

"Be back quickly, Mama!"

Agatha levels eye to eye with Krista, begging her daughter, "Remember. Do not open the door for anyone. I will stop at the back door and knock twice. Then I will knock twice again."

Agatha hugs her daughter, then covers her own head despite the heat with a cotton shawl. She steps out, closing the door. Krista reaches for the bolt and secures it.

Agatha looks left, then right, then walks toward the Beckmann rental home, all stone with three floors. It is larger than theirs. She spots Irma's younger sister, Sylvia, as she exits her own door, headed in the same direction. The five-point star on her breast looks wilted; her gait, defeated.

Agatha pauses mid-stride as it dawns on her that Sylvia is on her way to collect the month's rent. In a few minutes, they will be at the front door of the Beckmanns' together, and she will be ready with her own fee, as the tailoring shop is having a windfall courtesy of the new business they were receiving from Frankfurt. The news of Horst's skills as a tailor continues to keep them in comfort, though the meat, eggs and cheese are scarce at the market.

Sylvia raps on the Beckmanns' wooden door, which opens separately at the top, then the bottom, which has a separate latch.

Before Emma can open the door, Agatha greets Sylvia. "Good morning, Sylvia!"

Demurely, the woman looks back in deference after the incident at the train station. "Good morning."

Agatha knows and feels the guilt of the incident as if it only happened yesterday. To ease the woman, she tells her the rent is ready and offers for her to pick some vegetables from the garden. It is the least she can do if Sylvia is willing.

"Thank you, Agatha. I will come around. How is Mila?"

Agatha blushes in the awkwardness of the moment. Emma opens the top half of the door just as Mila's name is mentioned.

A pregnant pause. Agatha is not ready, although it was the sole purpose of her visit to the Beckmanns', but not with Sylvia listening.

Emma glances back at Agatha, expecting a reply, but is aghast at Agatha's reaction, plainly written on her face. "Agatha?"

"I'm sorry, Sylvia. Please, go ahead and conclude your transaction. I am intruding."

Agatha steps away as Emma hands Sylvia her fee. Sylvia pauses expectantly, waiting for a reply from Agatha, and feels the tension.

Emma looks back, her face beginning to show alarm. Agatha clarifies, "Emma, do you mind if I come in, please?"

Sylvia reads between the lines and steps away. "I must get going."

Agatha looks back, willing herself to not show her tears. "Please, Sylvia, when you have time, I mean it about the vegetables."

Sylvia nods and turns away.

14

EMMA OPENS the bottom latch of the front door, and Agatha bursts in, finally giving way to her tears.

"Please tell me! What happened!"

Emma's pinafore shows stains from beets, almost like blood. It conjures memories of what may have happened to Mila. Agatha looks at it and swoons.

Emma catches her friend and walks her to a chair. The door swings in the breeze, open to the noon heat.

"She's gone! My God, I am so sorry!"

"What do you mean? Who? Who is gone?!" Emma's horror and agony are plain on her face.

Agatha stands. "I saw Mila at the market. With a suitcase. She ran away from the house!"

Emma drops to the floor, prostate. "Why? Did something happen?"

Agatha looks out the window. "I think it's because Krista didn't want to go to the Youth Corps any longer. She was concerned someone there would catch us with Mila."

Emma stands up, emotions conflicted. She is grateful Agatha has hidden Mila all these years, but can't understand why Krista would discuss it with Mila in the room.

"She wasn't in the room, Emma. I sent her up to her bath. I needed a private moment with Krista, as she'd been troubled for a few days – but Mila must have overheard us."

"What was Krista saying?"

Agatha looked down. "That there is a labor camp she and this boy stumbled upon… and it bothered her so much, but it bothered her more that this boy found it funny. One of her pupils."

"And what was funny?"

"The way the soldiers were torturing and mocking people like Irma. And people like us who help children…"

"Like mine."

"Yes." Agatha looked pained.

Emma grabbed her sleeve. "Where is my daughter now? Where did they take her?!"

Agatha walks to the door. "The soldiers took her after some boy pointed her out. It might have been why Krista was scared for her… for us. The boy was about the age for the Youth Corps."

Agatha walked out the door as Emma followed. "I am going to get her."

Agatha whirled around. "I don't think you can. They put her in a black van for the laborers who were lined up."

Agatha walks away, Emma sobbing behind her, begging. "We can't just leave her there! Horst has to get her. He did before."

Agatha shakes her head, not willing anymore to save Mila and jeopardize her own family. She turns back, alarmed that the neighbors will hear, as they are outside the house. "Go back inside, Emma. They now know Mila is real. Go back and lock yourself in. I'm so sorry Mila overheard."

Agatha continues to stride towards her own house, willing herself to ignore Emma's pleas behind her. "So sorry?! So sorry?! How could you be so careless! You know how sensitive Mila is!"

Ahead of Agatha, Sylvia is standing under the sun, sweating, looking pointedly at Agatha. The young woman has a look of deep sorrow, fear and pity. She obviously heard everything from where she is standing.

Fear grows as Agatha approaches their own home. They have to hide just in case Mila gave them away as her refuge. She walks to the back door, Sylvia following behind her.

At the backyard, Agatha leans down and picks up a basket, handing it to Sylvia. "Whatever you can pick is yours. I'll be back in a few minutes."

Krista opens the back door in time for Agatha to knock. Agatha's stress is palpable. She yells at Krista, "I told you not to open it until I knocked!"

Krista reels back with the force of Agatha's yell. She leans against the wall as if attacked. "I'm sorry, Mama. I saw you and Sylvia before you knocked!"

Agatha grabs Krista by the arms, shaking her. "You have to listen when I tell you! Listen!"

Krista looks back in shock. "Yes, Mama. Yes."

"Listen!"

"Yes, I will listen."

Agatha turns away, surveying the house. She is taking in what she has to gather in preparation to flee.

A sharp rap on the front door. Then more loud knocking.

Agatha looks up, approaches the window, and sees two Gestapo in uniform standing expectantly by the front door.

She shoves Krista towards the stairs. Krista dashes up the steps as Agatha dashes out the back door in time to see Sylvia apprehended by two soldiers, her arms locked behind her by one, and the other holding her hair. As she struggles, the men laugh.

The front door slams open.

"Agatha Schneider!" A loud and angry male voice reverberates throughout the house.

15

Horst packs his briefcase, ready to depart for the day. The afternoon sun is now descending behind the building. The shadows of passersby on the ground in front pass the glass-fronted windows of the shop. Another tailor, his assistant, waves good evening and exits. The door dings once. Another customer?

Horst looks up to find another man, dressed in an SS uniform, a white armband on his sleeve, holding the door open. The man enters and clicks his heels in salute.

"Good evening, Herr Schneider."

Perplexed, Horst salutes back, his heels quiet.

The man smiles. "Brigadefuhrer Bayer has arrived." The man turns to open the door, and in comes the kommandant himself. The man is beaming.

Horst salutes again; this time his heels click.

The man removes his hat with the insignia of an eagle in gold. He sits by the tea table, the tea now cold. "I have the ideal house for you."

Horst takes it in. "Thank you, sir. I am deeply appreciative. But I have to discuss it with my wife."

"She will positively love the house. We can go there now, and you can see for yourself."

"Now, Kommandant?"

The man stands and gestures to the door, where the other soldier stands, opening it to the evening breeze. Horst doesn't feel he has a choice. He grabs his briefcase and exits with the brigadefuhrer in tow.

In the car, the brigadefuhrer is beaming, proud of his accomplishment. "I assure you that you will be very happy with this house. We have provided a housekeeper and washerwoman for your wife. She need not trouble herself with gardening vegetables any longer or washing clothes."

Horst takes in the input, realizing the man has been to their home or has sent someone there.

"Have you informed my wife?!" Fear creeps into Horst's voice unintentionally as his thoughts turn to the child who is in their home, hiding. Mila.

The kommandant reaches over from his side of the seat, patting Horst's hand in reassurance. "At this very moment, she is getting the surprise of her life."

Horst looks straight ahead, his jaw working. He begins to sweat and looks down at his briefcase.

"Would you like some refreshment? You look parched and hot, Herr Schneider."

Horst hazards a glance at the kommandant next to him, his hand reaching for a handsome leather-embossed picnic case. The case springs open to reveal scotch and glasses.

"Oh, no, thank you. I am fine."

16

Krista has just started rolling the wall of the hidden door shut that lead to the attic stair. Crouched down, she feels herself moving as if in slow motion as she hears two men outside laughing as Sylvia yells for them to let her go.

Then the front door below slams open, to her consternation, and she hears her mother's name called out.

She distinctly hears her mother's steps approach the door as she holds her breath.

"Mrs. Schneider, please. We are here to accompany you to see your new home."

"New home?! I'm sorry. I don't understand!"

"Please, your husband is on the way there as well to see it. By request of Brigadefuhrer Beyer."

"Oh! Really."

Krista hears her mother's tone change from terse to calm. It is almost a relief. Then her mother lets out a breath. "What is going on with our landlady?"

"Mrs. Schneider, she is no longer your landlady. You no

longer need to rent. The kommandant will explain, please. Follow me."

A pause.

"Please let her go."

The man walks heavily to the back door, and Krista hears it open.

"Men, let her go. We need to leave."

Laughter, spitting. Krista rolls the hidden wall open and emerges, sneaking up to the open window. Outside, the soldiers have let Sylvia go, but not so gracefully. She is lying on the ground as a soldier with a potbelly tosses her among the aubergines.

"Go ahead, sow. You can have some eggplants! Ha ha."

She sees her mother emerge, tossing a shawl around her shoulders. She looks up and makes eye contact with Krista, shaking her head.

Krista leans back into the room, apprehensive. Obviously, her mother doesn't want her to be seen. She dashes to her parents' bedroom across the way from Mila's old room and hazards a peek from the windowsill.

Outside, two men respectfully help her mother into the back of a black Mercedes, flags of the SS on either side of the car's front fender. Agatha is being escorted in style, but obviously she senses something afoot. As the vehicle pulls away, she sees her mother's face look out from the back seat, a man next to her offering a cigarette.

Krista recedes into the room and then bolts for the stairs.

Sylvia cleans off her hair, soiled with grass and mud

from the rough handling of the soldiers. She has some cuts on her arms and a large bruise on her forehead.

"Please, Sylvia, come into the house, and I'll clean those for you."

"You're so kind. Did your mother tell you what happened to Mila?"

Krista swallows. She is afraid to ask. She gestures toward the house, withdrawing a handkerchief with a pink peony embroidered on one end. Krista tenderly dabs Sylvia's wounds with it. "Come. Let's get inside, please."

At the kitchen table, Sylvia recounts what she overheard between her mother and Emma. She gasps as Krista applies alcohol swabs on her cuts. Expertly, Krista wraps the cuts on her head with a bandage and then the woman's arm.

Krista approaches the teakettle and fills it with water from the faucet.

"Please. Don't worry. I have to go, as they may come back here. I am sorry to say Mila might tell the soldiers where she was being hidden. Your parents cannot save her this time, as they need to save themselves."

Krista swallows. "I'm so sorry about your sister."

Sylvia looks back, almost in tears. "I guess we all have to do what we must do to save ourselves, right?"

Krista's face shows her compassion towards the woman who is so forgiving. She always felt they somehow betrayed Irma in order to save the Beckmanns, who were close friends.

"But now the SS must know. They just took my mother away."

Sylvia shakes her head. "No, you're moving out of here. The Gestapo needs your family, I think. They don't want you renting from a Jew."

"And what are you going to do? Where are we to go?"

"Your family will be comfortable. Me? I don't know. They let me go because your mother asked."

"And?"

"After that, I don't know. I will take it day by day." With that, Sylvia walks to the back door and turns and waves goodbye. "Good luck. I can't tell you where I'm going. It's better you know less."

She disappears.

Krista dashes to the door and watches Sylvia approach the hill behind the vegetable garden. Krista follows, stumbling past vines of grapes, a few lemon trees, and finally, up the crest of the hill, which protects their home from wind and gives them privacy. Sylvia's small figure is ambling towards a farmhouse in the distance. Beyond that, a wooded area that Krista has not noticed before.

Krista surveys the area, sees the road leading into the town where the market lies, the city hall where the Gestapo is now headquartered in their area, and the train station where Mila was caught. Krista sees the bread man and his son, now a teen, with his donkey and cart, returning from the market. He probably only had enough flour to make bread for the SS. These days, only the SS and their soldiers are a priority.

She turns around, eyeing their garden of vegetables and fruit trees. She approaches and notices for the first time the imprints of boots in the mud, the aubergines and lettuce flattened and trampled. The cabbages and turnips in a pile, trampled upon too and some smashed. Boot prints are everywhere. The soldiers have destroyed some of the plants. They were obviously meant for Sylvia to see as they were being moved out of there. Anger seizes Krista like a rolling train at midnight. Fast, loud and whistling with vehemence.

Krista enters the back door and shuts it, wondering who will come for her, trying to control her breath. *Where are we moving?* she wonders. *Where are my parents right now? Where is Mila? Will she betray us for her life?*

She dashes to the front window, past the kitchen table where the lemonade still sits, now warm, still waiting for Mila to drink it and smile her warm smile of simple gratitude.

The silence of the house deafens her. She feels a deep loneliness and is gripped by confusion and fear. She digs into her pockets, realizing her mother has given her the week's allowance for pulling weeds and tending to the watering of the garden. What WAS the garden. She counts the money and glances out the window.

17

HORST EXITS the handsome black Mercedes, the chauffeur appearing at the door in silence, holding it open. The kommandant has already ascended the short steps to a cream-colored stone house with blue shutters. Ivy trails the walls, with a large vine of wisteria crowning the entrance portico. Stunned, Horst cannot believe the size of the house and how it looks as if from a French storybook.

An older gentleman dressed in a butler's uniform opens the door, his waistcoat buttoned. He appears dapper, yet subservient. The man salutes, clicking his boots, as the kommandant and Horst enter the foyer.

The scents of lemon and verbena assail Horst's senses as he surveys the large foyer. On a table inlaid with marble sits a pale green celadon vase filled with an arrangement of blue irises, verbena and pink Gerber daisies. A portly woman stands nearby, looking prim and stern. She is wearing a standard Nazi uniform. She is buxom, hair pulled back, and looks strikingly familiar. She nods to acknowledge Horst without a smile.

Horst feels a chill despite the warm reception. The kommandant is speaking, but his eyes remain fast on the woman, who remains without emotion.

Then Horst remembers. She is the Youth Nazi recruiter who gave Krista her books, which were all for brainwashing the children whom Krista has to teach. Frau Dieter-something. Horst pretends nothing is amiss, now listening to his benefactor, who is showing him the parlor, then the large kitchen, the dining room, and finally the veranda beyond, facing the fields. He wonders where his wife is and is quickly answered when he hears a car arrive and park.

The brigadefuhrer claps his hands with gusto. "Ah! At long last your wife has arrived!"

They descend out to the patio lined with topiary bushes.

On the cobbled drive, Horst sees Agatha exit a vehicle identical to the one he exited several minutes before.

The buxom woman descends and intercepts Agatha, who is staring at the house in awe. Her response is similar to Horst's. She smiles at the buxom woman, whose name escapes her.

"Welcome. Your new home. You must remember me? Mrs. Schneider?"

Agatha surveys the woman's features and almost betrays a look of hostility. She quickly regains her composure. "Yes, of course. Frau Dieronstrasse?"

"No, Dieterstrasse. Your daughter is getting on very well."

Agatha manages to control her anger, recalling the conversation Mila overheard.

"Once she's settled here, I will have more mentoring to do. She is a quick study."

Agatha nods, shivering. The woman notices. "Stone homes tend to retain the chill. You will notice it once you enter."

The kommandant interrupts, escorting Agatha to the kitchen with the woman looking on, examining Agatha's back like a snake about to strike.

Horst follows Agatha, his teeth clenched.

The large French doors allow both air and light to enter from the patio into the dining area lavishly furnished with French provincial furniture in hues of cream and celadon green. Agatha can only imagine the room flowing with guests, but her disappointment shows in her face, as she knows the kommandant would not like her friends. The Beckmanns would be welcome here until the Gestapo discovers their daughter is Mila, who has just been caught and may even be fighting for her life in a camp as they speak.

Agatha tries to disguise her chagrin, especially from the observant eyes of Krista's mentor, Frau Dieterstrasse, whose name she preferred not to remember. Frau "Disaster", Agatha recalls. The woman is right behind them, Horst to her right, the kommandant to her left. Besides Horst, she feels surrounded by enemies who may soon discover how Mila managed to survive from a disabled child to a budding teen. That thought alone makes her wonder what Krista is doing while she is touring a well-appointed home fit for a baron. Again, her thoughts seem to have been read by the kommandant.

"Your daughter would love this room."

The butler, who is leading the way, ascends the carpeted stairs to a long hallway lined with a Turkish rug, which smells of wool. The rug is obviously new. The man turns the knob on the first door to the left to reveal a four-poster bed facing a French door, which is open to a large balcony. Beyond the large bed frilled with light green lace lies a bathroom with a beveled mirror.

All manner of stuffed toys, undoubtedly from Frankfurt, line a tall bookshelf in pale pink. The rest of the furniture is also of the same color and style. Very feminine and soothing. Agatha walks towards the bed, the thick Turkish carpet allowing her feet in the threadbare soles of her shoes to sink. She gasps in awe.

The butler points to the bathroom, which has a footed tub and a shower, two sinks and a bidet. It all looks French.

Agatha turns to the butler. "French furniture and fixtures?"

Before the butler can reply, the kommandant interrupts. "The previous owners were very fastidious and impeccable in taste, obviously. However, we changed the carpets, as they were soiled and old. Weren't they, Herr..."

The butler looks nervously at the kommandant. "Yes, sir. They are all new. Even some of the patio stones leading to the garden right below."

The kommandant gives the butler a stare, enough to

make the man wither. There is an uncomfortable pause as the man proceeds to an adjacent door, opening it for Horst and Agatha. "After you, Fraulein."

It is the master bedroom, which has a mauve ceiling, light pale pink walls, and masculine furniture in beechwood. The brass bed is huge. Agatha approaches it, touching the brass, and notes in horror that there are bloodstains on the brass railing of the floorboard. She shrinks away. Immediately, the butler wipes it with a handkerchief, which he withdrew from his own pocket. Agatha notes the man's hands are shaking as he furiously wipes at the stains.

Quickly, before Agatha or Horst can comment, the kommandant swiftly snatches the handkerchief from the butler, pocketing it. He turns apologetically to the couple, glaring at the butler as he speaks. "Sometimes the servants get sloppy. Someone was eating here and put gravy on the floorboard."

To the butler, the kommandant tersely issues a sharp bark. "Get a proper rag and wash it with cold water and soap."

The man dashes off as if he were hit.

"This way, please. Two more bedrooms for guests, and then we fetch your daughter."

Frau Dieterstrasse interrupts. "No need, sir. They are going to get her now. She will be here shortly."

The kommandant smiles at Frau Dieterstrasse. "Oh, good. She can join us for the – how do the French say it?"

"*Apéro*," Agatha ventures.

The kommandant gives Agatha a warm smile. "Yes.

Apéro. You fit the estate well. It was owned by a Jewish family who moved here from France."

Horst, naive as ever, ventures a question. "Where are they now?"

The kommandant clears his throat and looks away. "I would imagine they're on a train by now. Those who survived." He starts laughing and is joined by Frau Dieter-strasse.

18

A BANGING. Krista fell asleep, crying in her bedroom. She sits up, dashes to the window, and looks out at the garden below. She runs across to Mila's old room and hears the doorknob shake below. She leans over the sill and sees a black Mercedes, flags with the swastika flying in the breeze.

She pauses, wondering why the entourage.

A man down below in uniform looks up in time to catch Krista's eye. Krista gasps.

"Krista? Krista Schneider?"

She ducks.

"Come down, please. Your parents are waiting for you. Frau Dieterstrasse is also there."

Krista sits on the floor, conflicted. What if this is a trap? What would the Frau be there for?

Quickly, Krista digs in her pockets and reveals the meager cash her mother gave her the day before.

Down below someone shakes the door.

Krista bolts for Mila's room, pulling the curtains off the rods. She ties them together and descends from the window, reaching for a trellis that used to hold her mother's climbing vines, long dead.

Using the trellis and curtains like an improvised ladder, Krista clambers down, but a hand reaches for her.

She almost screams. It is Sylvia.

"You're back."

Sylvia puts a finger across her lips and tugs her to hurry. Krista follows her to the other end of the house, where the trestle tables, once laden with festive food on her birthday, lie. Leaves and twigs now litter the tops of the tables. Now just a memory, it seems long ago when she and Mila walked out into the group of cheering neighbors and friends to greet her on her special day. She remembers Mila's eyes covered in long bangs so as to prevent others from seeing her eyes, which betrayed her disability. She wonders now too if Sylvia will betray her presence and Mila's source of refuge in return for betraying Irma.

Too late. Krista is following Sylvia. She has to trust her until she is sure her parents are really safe. How can she find out? She thinks it through as they both sneak back towards the distant farmhouse. Surely her parents will return for her if everything is fine – or was this soldier sent to reunite her with them?

There is only one way to find out.

"Sylvia."

Sylvia turns, brushing the hair from her eyes. "The farmhouse is abandoned, and there is food in the cupboards. Hurry."

"I have to go back. I think the soldier is there to take me to my new house. My parents surely are there, as he said."

Sylvia looks on. "Are you sure they haven't found out about Mila?"

"No, I'm not sure. I don't know how else I would find out, though."

"What if your parents are being deported to the camps?"

"But, Sylvia, you said so yourself they were taking them to a house... away from here. You said you're free because of Mama."

"If you..."

"Sylvia, I appreciate your help, believe me. But I must find out what has happened to my parents. Either way, I want to be with them – house or camp."

"They're leaving." Sylvia gestures toward the black Mercedes, the men inside, pulling away from the house.

Krista stands, unsure. "I think I might be endangering you by being with you."

Sylvia pulls her down. "Please stay. If you decide to leave, you are free to go. I will protect you meanwhile."

Krista eyes the cotton star on Sylvia's breast. She wonders who is being protected.

"I will walk to town. If I see another soldier, I will ask where my parents are. If I see danger, then I will escape. At least I will know where we stand as a family."

"It's only a matter of time, Krista. Mila will talk in exchange for her life."

"I hope they allow her to live."

"They may not. They may also do something to your parents once they find out who kept Mila."

Krista, seized in conflict, appears tormented.

Sylvia gives her a brief smile. "Come on. Sleep on it. The town will be there tomorrow if you decide to go. The Gestapo has taken over, and it won't be that easy to get rid of them."

Convinced and in conflict, she allows Sylvia to lead her.

19

AGATHA OPENS one armoire after another laden with men's and women's clothing. Whoever lived there lived lavishly. Shoes line the floor, all made in high fashion and of quality. She turns to Horst, the sun fading outside. It is almost dinnertime.

"Where do you think Krista went?"

"The kommandant searched our house top to bottom. Surely they now know about the attic room – behind the washstand." This he says in a whisper.

Agatha shivers.

A timid knock. It is one of the soldiers.

"Herr Schneider, sorry to interrupt. The kommandant realizes that your daughter is missing and would like to take you back to locate her and get your belongings as well."

Horst looks on, pensive. "I'd like to ask that Agatha and I both go. Our daughter was taught not to go with anyone without us there. After all, she's only twelve."

"Yes, sir. The kommandant understands that. Are you ready to go in a few minutes, sir?"

"Please."

The couple exit the vehicle in front of their old home. Agatha looks up, already sensing Krista is not anywhere near the house. The soldier exits and stands near the couple.

"Why would she not go, Herr Schneider? The soldiers said she slipped out the window and down using the curtains to the back of the house. A strange way to accept living arrangements that are much better."

Defensively, Agatha offers an explanation. "She was not told, as we ourselves didn't know the surprise."

"Aren't surprises always good ones?" This is asked naively, without menace.

"Our daughter is an only child. She is extra cautious."

"She is German. No need to be cautious."

Horst and Agatha ignore the last statement and enter the empty house. They search the rooms, yelling Krista's name.

"Sir, if I may suggest, you gather what you may need for the evening and label the furniture for the movers. We will return with you tomorrow in the morning, and you can ask about your daughter's whereabouts."

Agatha glances back. "That's thoughtful of you, but we need only take our clothes. The house comes furnished."

"Again," the soldier says, "please feel free to take whatever furniture you need. The landlady won't be needing it."

This last statement sends shivers through Agatha's lithe frame.

She proceeds to open a cupboard and pulls out some clothing. Then she sees Mila's pinafore.

Tears well in her eyes.

Krista walks with tired feet, exhausted from walking through brush. Just a few yards away now, she spots the farmhouse, looking forlorn and abandoned in the late afternoon light. Ahead of her Sylvia trudges along, glancing back now and then to check on her.

Then the sounds of car motors. She glances back and thinks she hears her mother yelling. Then her father's voice.

"Krista! Krista!"

She stops. Turning, she spots her father at the open window of Mila's old room.

"It's safe. Come out!"

"Papa!"

Krista bolts for the house. Sylvia gives chase, trying to reach her. "Krista, no! It might be a trap!"

Krista is running as if her life depends on reaching her parents.

"No, Sylvia! I don't want to be apart from them! What will happen will happen!"

Krista runs to the crest of the hill, waving, yelling. Sylvia is right behind her.

"Papa! I'm here! Papa, don't leave!"

The soldier looks out the window next to Horst. "I see her, sir!"

Horst waves in joy. "I see you, sweetheart! I will come down and wait for you."

Sylvia pulls at Krista's dress, but she does not pause. Krista keeps running.

The soldier emerges with a rifle aimed at them.

Krista keeps running, as she sees Agatha looking out from another window.

Krista reaches the crest of the hill with Sylvia right behind her. Krista slips down the hill as Sylvia reaches the top.

A shot rang out.

Gunfire.

Sylvia screams, a gurgle.

Krista turns from her position on the ground.

Sylvia lies in a pool of blood, a hole right in the center of her chest. Her eyes glaze as a death rattle ensues.

"Oh God, no!"

"Krista!"

The soldier steps out with Agatha and Horst right behind him. They are rushing to meet Krista, who is getting up, looking at Sylvia on the ground.

"Someone help! Why?! Why?!"

Horst yells, "Get away, Krista. She's dead! She's gone!"

The soldier comes up, pulling the crying Krista up to her feet. She backs away from him, shocked at what he did to Sylvia. Agatha rushes up to hug her daughter.

"You almost shot my daughter!" Horst yells, alarmed.

The soldier feels for a pulse on Sylvia's wrist. Finding none, he kicks Sylvia's body away. "What matters is that your daughter is now safe from her. We can leave now."

Krista protests, “But she was protecting me!”

Both Agatha and Horst look on in alarm, but they look away, unable to protest. Krista searches her mother’s face in tears.

“Mama, where are we going now?”

The soldier yells at Krista: “Come! It grows late. The house is waiting.”

Another soldier stands by the open Mercedes. It sounded like an order.

The family walks away from Sylvia’s body and towards the waiting car. Krista looks back at Sylvia’s body as they head for the car and into a new life. She feels numb.

20

Krista lies on the canopied bed, feeling the satin sheets enveloping her. She puffs up the soft pillow in a shade of pastel blue with pink florets. She pauses, listening. Eventually, she turns to the French windows and hides her body under the sheets as she looks at the balcony beyond, the wrought-iron filigree pattern reminiscent of a house she used to admire in Frankfurt.

Trouble furrows her brows, her nerves on edge from witnessing Sylvia being shot in her tracks as she tried to reach Krista. The young woman was attempting to protect her and died doing so. Both sisters, Irma and Sylvia, were good landladies. Good German citizens whose sense of integrity prevailed until the very end. Now they are both dead, and here she is, lying in a bed, living in a house that doesn't belong to them. The house doesn't belong to the Nazis either. It was taken from a family struck down and murdered because of who they were.

Krista sits up. She looks at the beautiful French

provincial clock on the mantelpiece near her, a study in cream and gold. It reads 2 a.m. She can't sleep. She feels her young heart thumping in her chest. She could have saved Sylvia's life if she had followed her to the farmhouse and slept there until morning. Then leaving Sylvia there, she could have walked into town on her own, finding out about Mila or her parents. Sylvia would have been alive, until she could have moved on to another hiding place. Without Krista, she had no one to protect.

Krista swings her feet to the polished floor. It gleams and smells of fresh lemon. Padding softly across the Persian carpet to grab her robe, which is also new, she wraps it around her thin frame and edges quietly toward the door of her new bedroom. The beauty and elegance of the feminine room, accented with small cherubim painted at the edges of the ceiling, does nothing to soothe Krista. Its quiet beauty is lost on her as she mourns Mila and Sylvia, both lost within a space of days to a tragic end. Does beauty matter in a space of serenity where there is injustice? She could be in the midst of a slum and be happy if she knows her friends are all around her.

But then she thinks, *I'm twelve*. Every twelve-year-old needs her friends. Right now, most of her friends are "teaching" younger students the same books she still has to use. She just couldn't bring herself to use them until one afternoon Frau Dieterstrasse asked one of her charges a "rule" that is in the book. The poor kid had no idea and began to try, then, perceiving failure, cried. Krista swiftly came to the rescue, indicating that the child was not there when they were discussing that chapter. Krista thought the

Frau would let it go at that, but later, she got a stern lecture about the importance of tutoring the children who got left behind when absent.

Krista picks up one of the books now, piled high on a desk that looks very feminine and tasteful. She feels dwarfed by the bedroom and marvels at the warmth of the room due to its pastel colors. Bright and airy, she likes it and looks forward to inviting her friends to the topiary garden, which needs no maintenance from her, as the previous tenants' gardener was retained.

Tears come to her eyes as she wonders about Mila, feeling alone and probably in fear for her life. She throws the book against the settee by the window, the upholstery matching the bedspread, the other chairs in the room, and a section of the wallpaper. It is lavish beyond her own imagination. She wishes Mila could see it all, be right next door, playing and singing in a low voice as she did every morning.

Krista steps into the bathroom, her very own, and marvels at the thick Turkish towels hanging and waiting for her.

She reaches for the gold knob of the shower, twists it, and a warm flow of water issues from the spigot above. No more heating water for her bath.

Magic.

Krista luxuriates in the warmth, then turns it to cool so she can awaken. Stepping out onto the cool tile, she reaches for the plush towel and fastens it around her, hair dripping.

At the large mirror of the dresser, she looks back at her

reflection, then reaches for her old comb, a plain tortoise-shell affair her mother purchased when she was seven years old.

The large beveled mirror gilded in gold filigree reflects a large armoire behind her, cream colored and also gilded in gold.

Krista turns, now curious, eyeing her unopened luggage, which was hastily packed before she could even say goodbye to the neighbors.

Then she looks at the armoire. Opening it, she marvels at the clothes. It seems filled with fine clothing for a girl about her age. She feels herself starting to enjoy it, like a candy store in the middle of August. Playfully, she closes her eyes and decides she will arbitrarily pick out what she wants to wear that day, as there are numerous dresses.

Eyes shut she reaches out her hand among the clothing lined up on hangers. Left to right, then, finally, she reaches in.

Inside the armoire, a pale feminine hand, about the size of her own, hands her unsuspecting hand a hanger – a blue pop-sleeve dress with a prim neckline and empire waist.

Her hand secure around the hanger, Krista's eyes pop open, and she grins with approval. It is perfect.

21

AGATHA LOOKS THROUGH THE CUPBOARDS, all fitted and connected to the walls all around the brightly lit kitchen with beamed ceilings. Like her old kitchen, the windows let in the air and sunlight, but for some reason, she feels a distinct chill even on the hot summer morning. A truck is coming at noon with Horst riding with the driver, a soldier or two appointed to help the family move the rest of their belongings. There is really little furniture to move, and she is glad for that, as the house already has some handsome furnishings she and Horst always hoped to have with the rising fame of his tailoring skills.

Now they have all the furniture they wanted, and she wonders at what cost it comes. She truly hopes it is not at the cost of someone's life or misfortune.

Agatha feels very conflicted and saddened that Mila will not see nor benefit from their instant luxury, and that it cost Sylvia her life, just like it did with Sylvia's older sister, Irma.

She plans on going into town, now an easy walk from the other end of Bleichenbach, where they are now surrounded not by farmers' fields, but a street with lights and cobbled walkways separate from the village street. She will miss their vegetable garden in the back of the house and the villagers, especially the Beckmanns.

The Beckmanns. She must check on Emma and see if she has heard from or seen Mila. She asked Horst about paying a visit, but he sternly cautioned against any further contact for the moment, as the Gestapo and the brownshirts in the village may be watching for any talk of Mila. Especially the Nazi youth, since one child gave Mila away.

Krista enters the kitchen, crisp in the new dress from the armoire. She eyes the Danishes on the counter, the coffee pot, and the large pitcher of milk. She sits, still adjusting to the opulence of the room, noting the silence in the absence of her father and Mila. Agatha seems to be reading her thoughts.

"Your father got up early to return to the house to get the rest of our things. A soldier with a truck collected him this morning."

Krista pours herself a glass of milk, the cream from it lining the upper half of the glass. She reaches for a Danish filled with cheese, but she does not have much of an appetite. She munches, thinking of what chores to do, as there is a washerwoman outside the back door, looking through the laundry.

It is a Sunday, and she normally helps her mother do the laundry and hang it out to dry. The woman, a thin and pale lady, is wearing a brown outfit. Obviously a "brownshirt" – civilians recruited to spy on other civilians to ascertain their loyalty to the Reich. The thought makes Krista shiver. She makes a mental note not to trust the woman or engage in any conversation that may jeopardize them.

Agatha busies herself making lime juice as Krista eats in silence. Agatha turns to watch the washerwoman enter and toss the large and empty wicker basket that held the dirty laundry onto the kitchen floor. The woman exits the back door, nods towards Agatha without a word, and shuts the door behind her. Soon, they hear splashing as their clothing is being washed by hand.

Krista makes eye contact with Agatha, who then nods knowingly.

Agatha walks towards the windows near the back door where the woman is outside, and proceeds to silently close the shutters. Krista overhears her explaining, "It keeps it cool," which Krista knows is for the benefit of the washerwoman, who may be listening. The sunlight is coming in from the back.

Agatha walks back towards Krista, still whispering. "I was thinking of going into town just to see if there's any information on Mila's whereabouts."

Krista looks up in alarm. "No, Papa forbade us..."

"I know."

"But, Mama."

"Okay. Let's unpack today, and I will see about tomorrow or the next day. Better?"

"I will be in school, then the youth classes."

"You don't need to go with me. It may be best if I am alone."

"What if you see Emma? She will want you to help. She might get emotional again, as you said."

"We shall see."

22

KRISTA AWAKENS to the distinct tone of feminine singing. She sits up and looks to her left, outside the open window. Night. A breeze billows the curtains. A scent of honeysuckle fills the air. She isn't sure what awakened her, but she feels her skin prickle.

Then a faint girl's voice, singing. Whatever it is is in German. A tune she isn't familiar with. Standing, she steps with naked feet onto the wooden floor, clean and gleaming with polish. She walks tentatively to the window and looks out. All is peaceful and silent. Whoever it is, the singing suddenly stops.

In the corner of her eye, she thinks she sees a shadow of a dark-haired girl in a nightgown similar to hers. The figure is standing by the open French doors, which lead out to a balcony facing the front of the house, over the driveway. It looks for a minute as if it is headed for the balcony. She looks down and realizes she is wearing the same nightgown. Krista touches the nightdress, sensing it belonged to someone else. She then realizes in her haste to get to bed and in the stress of the first day at the house, she meant to put on her own old nightdress and instead picked this nightgown up.

Yes, it isn't hers. It is someone else's, and now she senses from the vision that it doesn't belong to her.

Quickly, still filled with unease, Krista pulls the nightgown over her head, clutching at her naked shoulders as she approaches the dresser in search of her old nightdress. Opening the top dresser, she rummages, and then she hears the singing again. Quickly now, she finds it, pulls it on, and turns to head for the door of the room.

Behind Krista, the breeze blows in from the balcony through the open French doors. Behind the doors, a distinct feminine face of a child of twelve like Krista, but with dark brown hair.

Then it vanishes.

"Mama. Mama."

Krista timidly knocks at the door to her parents' bedroom, embarrassed. She is twelve, going on thirteen. Inside, she hears a rustle of sheets, feet on the hardwood floor. The door opens. It's her father, his hair standing on end, eyes sleepy and taking in her expression.

He opens the door to let her in without a word.

Agatha sits up, arms wide in welcome. "Come."

Krista rushes to her parents' bed, a large wrought-iron affair with tall filigreed posts. Agatha makes room without a word, putting an arm around her daughter, sensing her unease as the girl snuggles.

"There was some girl in my room, Mama."

Horst chuckles. "Nightmares bring us together."

Agatha qualifies with apprehension, a believer of ghosts. "I had a dream too. There was a woman by the dresser, combing her hair."

"It was just a dream, Agatha," Horst qualifies.

Krista looks back at her father. "I was awake. It was a girl wearing a nightgown that I had taken from the dresser. I took the gown off."

Agatha sits up, looking down at her husband. "Let's get rid of their clothing. It isn't right to be here in their home in the first place."

Horst pulls himself up, now sensing the unease from both. "We have to appear gracious towards the Nazis, but I think it's safe to just put their clothes away in the attic. Just in case the owners come back."

"Horst, dear, that WAS blood I saw on this iron bed."

Krista looks back like she's been shot. "Blood?!"

"Now you did it, Agatha. We talked about not letting her know."

"Know WHAT, Papa?!"

Agatha steps out of the bed, sitting on an easy chair nearby. It is time to disclose what she saw that was hastily wiped off by the butler.

Horst reaches over, hugging his daughter. "Your mama and I were walking through with the butler and one of the soldiers who escorted us here. Your mom saw what she thought was blood at the foot of the bed. The railing." He points with his mouth. Krista gets up, moves over to the footboard and examines the railing.

"It's been wiped off, honey. The butler cleaned it. It

might have been someone who accidentally scratched themselves."

"Horst..."

"Let's not make what might be a simple explanation more complicated."

"But, Horst... why are all the carpets new?"

Horst gives his wife a look. "You're reading too many novels and listening to those radio shows."

"Not if you knew what's happening in Poland."

Krista senses the tension. "I can't sleep."

Agatha gets up, putting on her robe. "I'm going to start unpacking some boxes and getting breakfast ready. I don't want to rely on a housekeeper."

Horst glances at the clock on the night table near him. "Krista, go help your mom unpack, as you're awake anyway. Then prepare for school. Let's not let one night make our day difficult."

Krista looks at the clock near her father. 4:44 in the morning.

She feels her father's hand on her head, comforting. "Let's make the best of it. You tell me anything else you see or sense, okay?"

Downstairs, Krista hears the back door being unlocked. The butler has arrived.

23

KRISTA WALKS the new route to school, joining a few of her classmates in the same Youth Corps uniform of spring: khaki shorts, a white blouse and vest, and a short khaki necktie that has a pin of the Nazi swastika in red. Now living in an upscale neighborhood, she recognizes where some of her more "entitled" classmates live, now that they are neighbors. They are all turning thirteen, some are already, and some are flirting with boys who live in the same area. Most in this neighborhood are children of colonels, lieutenants, generals and the like. Long titles in German she'd just as soon forget about.

She is going to be civil, friendly even, to keep up the pretext for her parents' sake. She hates being German because of the Nazis. Her father told her in no uncertain terms that she is not to express her political views anywhere outside the house or even around the washerwoman, housekeeper, and the silent butler.

The washerwoman. Prim and steadfast, the woman is

subservient to Agatha, but she hardly speaks and at times exudes a vibe bordering on disdain. Was she there when the Jewish family lived there, or was she recently placed there only to spy on them? Krista realizes she can hardly recall her name. It could be fake, like the fake smiles she receives from some of her classmates, who now march in front of her as they near the school building's grayish facade. Boring, uncreative, almost like a mausoleum.

She walks up the steps, carrying her books, two of which are for the youth group later that afternoon. This time, she decides she is taking them on a trip to a local museum of artifacts and then sitting under the trees by the museum courtyard. No one will hear her telling her funny stories harvested from years with people who lived as a simple community on the other side of Bleichenbach. Her real home with real people who love to laugh and share jokes.

Krista thinks of her mother as she enters and dutifully raises her right hand in salute to the headmistress, a woman without comment nor power in an age of corruption and cronyism.

Mama. What is her day like on this Monday in this new neighborhood? Perhaps easier, as the butler and housekeeper are there for her.

Agatha walks swiftly in the early morning, turning to glance back at the fading figure of her daughter as the girl briskly walks to school. She decided she wouldn't divulge to her family that she is walking to the market square today to see what she can find out.

Agatha is very troubled by Mila's situation and feels

obligated to Emma Beckmann, her friend. She had to convince herself that there is no trouble checking into the situation and paying a visit to an old friend. She misses her. She could confide in Emma and feels a passive resistance and a distancing from the new neighbors despite her newness. Horst told her to give them a chance despite the political differences and the stark differences in values.

Whereas the Schneiders value a simple and humble lifestyle, such as a simple walk in the park, with an emphasis on good fresh food, the new neighbors purchase clothes from the latest Paris fashions even after ration cards were issued and they invaded Poland. This area, obvious from the house they are in and the opulence of the gardens in the neighborhood, has a penchant for a lavish lifestyle, from furnishings to art. Horst's dresser and closet, the latter the size of a small child's bedroom, is filled with fancy new shirts, coats, hats and shoes all polished. The heels had yet to touch the ground.

To make matters more difficult, Krista has nothing in common with the children, and she is turning into a teen. Teens need their friends. *However, she is doing her best*, Agatha thinks. *Why can't I, as I am her mother?*

Agatha turns the corner, and suddenly the open square is ahead of her. From this new vantage point, she is approaching from the quieter side, with the large establishments on her right and the outdoor cafes on her left further up. A public park is immediately near her, which probably accounts for her surprise, as it is a much quieter area with the alcove of trees exuding a serene and more restive atmosphere. Much quieter than her approach from the other end of the village where they used to live.

Immediately, she sees a few soldiers in Gestapo uniforms sitting and mingling at a cafe, obviously having breakfast. Tendrils of cigarette smoke issue from their table as a mild-mannered young man in his twenties busily tends to them. Agatha envies their ease despite what they are doing to the townspeople who don't fit so-called "Aryan" characteristics. She thinks they should at least feel guilty, but she knows that will never happen.

She walks determinedly towards the stalls of food and provisions, hoping to catch someone she knows from the old neighborhood.

And shortly, she does. It is none other than Emma.

"Emma!" She hears her own voice yelling over the din of haggling sellers and customers.

Emma appears bedraggled, her frayed clothing showing so clearly in contrast to the new dress Agatha chose to wear despite her nightmare. After all, it was still wrapped and never worn, she reasoned, after boxing the rest with the help of the butler. Clothing is one of the few pleasures Agatha denied herself when Horst was still a tailor's apprentice.

Emma eyes her friend with a tinge of envy and pain. She is about to avoid her; however, her desire to find out what may have happened to Mila wins out. She walks over, tugs Agatha away from a nearby produce stall, and whispers, "Have you talked to Horst? About my daughter?"

Agatha shakes her head. She is there for precisely the same reason.

Emma searches Agatha's face, as if it will betray some information to the contrary. "You've got to find out, Agatha. Surely there's a way for you or Horst..."

Agatha shakes her head, looking at the stalls as if shopping. "Let's talk privately. I was here to see if I would hear anything..."

"Nothing. I've been here for a while now."

Agatha tugs at Emma's arm, trying to move her away from the market. "I think we should have some coffee somewhere..."

"What happened to Sylvia?"

Agatha pauses and offers, "We could do nothing. She was a Jew."

Emma's body stiffens, her fists clenched around an old basket. "But Mila is NOT a Jew! She is not like Sylvia! We CAN do something! YOU can do something!"

Agatha realizes too late that the walk to locate Emma was a mistake. Hastily, she strides away and makes for an obscure street in the direction of her new neighborhood. Emma follows as she glances at the street sign.

"I see! So, this time you traded Sylvia's life so you could live among the entitled! I see how quickly we..."

Agatha swiftly turned, confronting her accuser. "I didn't trade anyone's life. She was shot before we could get to her. Mila was taken BEFORE I COULD GET TO HER!"

Emma starts crying. "You traitor! You gave her up without a fight!"

Agatha slaps her.

Emma recoils in shock.

Agatha whispers through clenched teeth, "I took Mila

in at the cost of jeopardizing my own family! For several years..."

A soldier who had been watching across the street crosses and confronts the two women. "*Zig heil!* Who is betraying who?"

Emma starts laughing the laughter of someone who is on the edge of hysteria. "YOU don't want to know!"

The soldier pointedly looks at Emma, then Agatha. "I believe I do, Frau..."

Emma stands tall. "Beckmann. Mother of Mila Beckmann. She was taken by your Gestapo."

Agatha reels back, stunned in disbelief by Emma's statement.

"Who is this Mila, and why would we take her, Frau Beckmann?"

Agatha is now beyond appalled. She attempts to rescue the situation. "My friend is distraught. She is confused. She has no daughter."

The soldier examines Emma, noting her dress. Then he looks at Agatha, noting her fine garment. "Your domestic help, Frau...?"

"Frau Schneider. No, she's a friend."

"WAS a friend," qualifies Emma. "She let my daughter be taken..."

Agatha's flushed face betrays her fears. The soldier notices and holds on to both their arms on either side of him. His hands are a viselike grip as he forcibly escorts them towards a building with the SS flags. Another soldier approaches, sensing he needs assistance. The man grabs Emma's arm as she attempts to pull away.

"Ladies, we're taking you to headquarters. You can have your discussion there."

"Good. You've taken my daughter! I want her back!" Emma's face is contorted in anger.

The man looks back in surprise. "Please, Frau Beckmann, we will look into this."

Emma looks up at the building, yelling her daughter's name for all to hear. "Mila! Mila! Mila!"

24

"Mila! Mila! Mila!"

Horst shakes Agatha awake, her face sweating, her hair matted as she lies on the pillow. It is night, and they are in bed.

Agatha looks relieved as she acknowledges she's safely in bed next to Horst in the new house.

"Please, let me get you some water." Horst shuffles out of bed, untangling himself from the sheets. The door latches shut as Agatha lies back.

Above her, the reflection from the streetlight on the ceiling fades. Then a face materializes, all bloody and bruised, one eye missing.

It is Mila.

Agatha screams.

The face disappears.

Running feet.

A door whooshes open.

Krista rushes in. She reaches for her mother. Downstairs, a shuffling, then a thumping up the steps.

Horst returns with a glass of water, the water sloshing as he shakily pauses over the bed. "What happened?!"

Agatha sobs. "I saw Mila. She's gone. Mila's gone."

Tears well in Krista's eyes.

Agatha sips the glass of water and hands it back to Horst. "I will tell you my dream, Krista. Before the servants awaken, I will tell you both."

In the hallway, standing by the bedroom door, the butler listens silently. He turns on his heel and shuffles away, putting his spectacles back in his pocket.

The butler walks down the back stairs and enters the kitchen, briskly walks through it and out the door. He walks past the wall clock as he exits. It is 11 p.m. He stayed longer than he meant to. Just in time for him to hear Frau Schneider screaming. He was marveling at how village families from the rural part of town went to bed so early at 9 p.m. The previous family didn't even eat dinner until 8 p.m., then some music and radio broadcasts were prohibited, which left the family reading books. When that family listened to the radio anyway, he just had to report it. Then, to his regret, they were taken away. *Well*, he thought, *I was just doing my job.*

He steps out into the cool night air and starts walking home, suspicion mounting in his head with each passing block.

Who is Mila? Why was Frau Schneider having a nightmare about her?

It is midnight in a wood, dark as pitch except for

wolves' eyes glinting in the distance. They are running quietly in packs. One howls the howl of death. They stalk and stop behind a copse of trees.

In a clearing, a line of women and some children, shivering in wet clothing. They are standing with their backs to a creek. There is a surreal feel to the line of people. Most are disabled with crutches, legs deformed; some are clearly manifesting some form of disability. Most of the women are murmuring in distress, some crying, some in shock. At the end of the line stands Mila, her face a mirror of terror. She is hugging her shoulders despite the humidity and keeps looking behind her at the creek. Her face is all bruised, and blood has matted her blonde hair, which hangs over her eyes.

Soldiers are lined up a few feet away, facing them, boots glinting like the wolves' eyes that stand awaiting several yards uphill. From her vantage point, Mila can see both the soldiers staring, with their rifles raised and pointed at them, one at her, and the wolves watching behind the soldiers.

She closes her eyes as the order is given.

Guns fire.

The rivulets of water in the creek mingle with blood, racing together through the forest.

The howling resumes.

25

HORST FOLDS the newly completed outfit. A woman's dress in burgundy with a sailor's collar, the skirt narrow-waisted like the fashion of the day. He dusts it with a fine brush meant for the fine houndstooth fabric. It is a fall dress. He arranges it on a hanger and positions it near another outfit, glancing out the storefront window to check another tailored men's suit. He catches Agatha walking on the opposite sidewalk across the street, past the market where she usually goes. Curious, he walks over to the glass door and sees her cross towards the more rural area of the village. She is obviously headed for their old neighborhood.

He muses, concerned. He makes a mental note to ask her about her trip when they sit down to dinner, wondering if the nightmare has prodded her to check in with Emma. His intake of breath is unmistakable as he furrows his brows in worry.

KRISTA GRABS her books from the school desk, almost forgetting the last two: the teachers' youth books for her pupils. The Reich propaganda from Frau Dieterstrasse. She almost lets out a chuckle, as she is not going to be covering any "material" on the Reich today. She has mentally run through the stories and jokes from the old village and in her mind's eye has a vision of the children laughing at her jokes in the garden outside the museum.

THAT BOY, the ten-year-old who delighted in watching soldiers inflict pain, is sick and out again. Roll call was heaven today, knowing he would not be there to possibly snitch on her and spoil the fun by dwelling on negative things. Maybe that is his karma – an eye for an eye for not having compassion.

Krista feels a pang of guilt for wishing thoughts that are not like her. She feels a well of anger deep inside for having to put up with him and the Frau, who snatched her life from her by pushing books she was forced to use. Then they had to leave their friendly village for a handsome neighborhood that has no life, but for the well-tended gardens.

Krista could go on and on ruminating on these negative thoughts, making her feel worse as her stomach responds with a gurgle.

Then, as Krista exits the schoolroom to collect the

pupils she has instructed to wait for her at the portico's garden path, she spots Frau Dieterstrasse, all three hundred buxom pounds of her, thumping her way towards Krista.

The woman looks furious.

DETERMINED, Agatha clutches her basket as she weaves her way into the narrower streets towards her old neighborhood. The familiarity of the smaller homes and humble gardens, well-tended by loving hands, makes her feel comforted. With every step, she feels her movements become more fluid, as if something is renewing her vigor. The new house drains her of energy. It feels foreboding, cold, unwelcoming. She turns into another street and sees the long lane leading to her old neighborhood at the edge of the village, leading to the farms that border the homes.

BY A WINDOW, a ten-year-old boy, miserable and appearing sullen, sits watching her. It is the boy from Krista's group of Youth Corps pupils. Krista unconsciously forgets his name, but it is Walter – the same boy with the freezing light blue eyes whose steely look only gives in to mirth and laughter when he sees pain. He is home, as Krista was told, recovering from illness.

As Agatha approaches her old neighborhood, the loudspeakers watching her from above like hawks, she fails to detect a boy following her. Feigning illness, the boy Walter managed to stay home. Now, idleness and boredom betray him as he slithers like a snake, stealthily hiding as Agatha pauses mid-stride to take in her old neighborhood, seeking solace with familiarity and the desire for friendship with old bonds.

In the school hallway, Krista pauses midstep, clutching her books, seeking escape.

Perhaps the woman will pass by her on a different mission.

No.

Frau Dieterstrasse, her portly figure heaving with the effort of her harried mission, stops dead center in the hall.

Agatha arrives and knocks on Emma Beckmann's door, resolute on forgiveness and solace from the hate that is accumulating around her. She interprets the nightmare as a reason to resolve the apprehensions that appear to beg for resolution.

As if Emma is waiting, the door opens, and Emma's face mirrors her own relief.

THE SUN STREAMING from the windows along the right make Frau Dieterstrasse's blonde hair look like a halo around her evil head.

It makes Krista wince with the irony of it as she passes the woman.

"I need a word with you before you go further!"

Krista's lips form an O.

EMMA STANDS AT THE THRESHOLD, hugging her friend.

Agatha, unable to contain herself, begins to talk, seeking reparation. "I wanted to see you. I wanted to see if by some miracle Mila had been released!"

Walter stands by an ancient water well, pretending to retrieve a bucket at the bottom, just steps from the Beckmanns' front door.

FRAU DIETERSTRASSE PULLS KRISTA ASIDE, away from students who are leaving, who watch and rush off to avoid the buxom woman's detection.

The Frau glares down at Krista. "I need YOU to stay in your room and pack your things when you get home."

"Why?! We just got there."

Emma starts to cry, already distraught. She has lost weight and has an unhealthy pallor, Agatha observes.

"I would only pray even more if there was hope."

"Has anyone seen her?"

"No. She's probably in a labor camp."

Agatha hugs her friend, whose knees have buckled in reaction. Emma holds on to her as Agatha attempts to usher her inside the house.

"You stupid girl! You will be living with ME!"

Krista looks back, eyes astonished. "No, I will not!"

Dieterstrasse slaps her.

Emma, distraught, grieving, gives in to her agony as they stand at the front door. "She's gone! We tried, Agatha! She's disabled, and too many people know!"

Walter's eyes become as round as saucers. He backs away, dropping the bucketful of water. Agatha hears the bucket fall and splash. She turns in time to see the figure of a boy running down the lane.

Emma looks on in surprise, following Agatha's gaze. Agatha looks back at her friend in consternation. "Get inside, quick!"

"STAY in your room and pack until you're told otherwise."

"Why do I have to live with you?!"

The Frau appears as if she has been slapped. "Your mother and her friend have conspired to keep a non-Aryan!"

With that, the Frau pushes a frayed black-and-white photo into her hand. It is a picture of Mila and Krista taken inside the rental home on the morning of Krista's birthday party. Mila's bangs disguise part of her eyes, but it is clear she has Down's syndrome.

26

VEINS STAND out of Brigadefuhrer Beyer's face, pulsing. He is furious. Horst sweats profusely as he watches Beyer pace the shop, his boots thumping against the fine wood floor.

The man pauses at eye level with Horst, who is forced to look away. The vehemence burns through him.

"Your wife, Herr Schneider, has been conspiring to hide a mongoloid child! For several years, I might add!"

Horst is speechless.

"YOU have nothing to say?! You knew. You boldly lied about this child! This mongoloid!"

"Sir, I... I had no doubt..."

The kommandant yells back, "You KNEW, as the Beckmanns were your friends! You knew you were lying to the Reich!"

Horst is trembling, clutching with sweaty hands a shirt meant for the brigadefuhrer. The fabric is now wrinkled.

The man snatches the shirt from Horst's hands and issues an order. "You are being moved to the army installation of OUR choice, Herr Schneider! There, you will make uniforms day and night of the same quality as before."

"What about my daughter?!"

"She's being taken to Frau Dieterstrasse's home. Away from you and your influence. She is already becoming a good Aryan – without you."

"Please! Please!"

"As for your wife... she is going on the next train to Dachau with her best friend Frau Beckmann."

Horst feels something hot travel down his pants.

The kommandant looks down to discover a tendril of urine traveling towards his boots. The man hits Horst.

Horst falls to the ground, sitting in a pool of liquid that is his urine.

"Don't you dare find out where Frau Dieterstrasse lives. You will not be allowed to even know where YOU are!"

27

Krista packs two large suitcases, the butler allowing her to take some of the new unused clothing from the previous owner's family. Her hands shake, her head swims, as she distractedly looks at the butler and housekeeper, who both pull out clothing from each drawer.

Krista goes through the previous week's events, trying to recall how the soldiers got a hold of the photograph in the rental house. They must have searched for it, but why? Did Mrs. Beckmann indiscreetly discuss Mila without regard for her mother's safety after they departed? Did she feel so betrayed by Agatha that she gave up her own friend to bargain for Mila's return? Krista's head spins with a million theories and questions, but she is so distraught that she keeps packing and unpacking the same suitcase.

Finally, the housekeeper, a lithe young woman in her thirties who appears kind and quiet, intervenes and tells her to sit as she packs for her. Krista is grateful, as she feels her heart throb in pain and anxiety for her parents. She wonders about her father. Has he been arrested? What will happen to his shop? Only one person may know.

The washerwoman, or the brigadefuhrer himself.

She will try the washerwoman, then as much as she dreads it, the kommandant himself.

If Frau Dieterstrasse allows it.

Frau Dieterstrasse is in a white Audi. She is behind the wheel, which is new to Krista. In her lifetime so far, Krista had yet to see a woman driving a car. Krista emerges from the side door leading to the kitchen with the young housekeeper carrying a basket of bread.

The butler emerges with Krista's luggage, all bound in leather, a testament to the previous homeowner, who outfitted the house, the garden and furnishings, let alone their clothing, with great care and panache. Krista feels exhausted, grieving and sick to her stomach. She has lost Mila, now her own mother and, possibly, her father as well. Now, she is losing a beautiful house and its ghosts, whose secrets will never have a chance to be revealed. She recalls in her mind's eye the young girl whose nightdress she wore.

How Krista longs to be reunited with her parents again. How she misses the rental house with the funny and high-spirited landlady sisters, Irma and Sylvia, now dead because of who they were. She looks at the house's handsome facade from the side, bidding another farewell to the short stay, which leaves her haunted by their ghosts, and hoping, hoping, longing and wishing that her parents and Mila will be restored to her. To live in this house. This beautiful house with its painful secrets.

No, Krista decides she doesn't want a house that rightfully doesn't belong to her or her parents. They, like her family, were torn asunder and made to suffer for being in the right. For not knowing how evil Germany has become under the Reich.

The Frau gestures from the car, her brows knitted, her hands pointing to the seat next to her. She obviously means Krista. The housekeeper, to Krista's surprise, quickly hugs her, a stranger with a kind face. The young woman hands her the basket of fresh rolls and pastries, still warm and inviting.

The butler has her possessions in the large boot of the car and has slammed it shut for the benefit of Krista. Like a signal it is to her – to depart forever the only village she has ever known.

Tearfully, Krista descends the few steps with the basket, the butler opening the door with a cold but fearful look, as if he will find an answer in the distance where his eyes stray. She wants so much to run. Run back to the house and lie in her parents' bed, where the sheets are probably still warm from the night before.

As she sits next to the buxom woman, Krista looks back at the slim housekeeper, who gives a wave of sadness, of defeat. The butler stands at attention, dutifully awaiting the car to roll away to Krista's next home.

Krista looks out the window, clutching the basket of rolls, her stomach gurgling. She closes her eyes, willing herself to sit back and let the susurrus of the engine lull her to calm. However, it is not to be.

Krista's eyes fly open as she hears the voice of a young

girl, the same girl from the night before. Krista glances at the Frau, who appears concentrated on her driving as they putter past the neighborhood replete with birch and elms. She hears a feminine young voice say, "Look," in her mind, and she looks at the rearview mirror.

Reflected from the back seat is a face that looks familiar to Krista. The frilly collar, the small shoulders. She wore that nightgown just the night before, unwittingly not knowing its owner would object. Now she's here... with her... in the handsome car. Krista shuts her eyes, then looks again. The girl is definitely there, silent, signaling as if willing herself to communicate a need. A message.

Krista keeps staring, then realizes. She must keep track of where they're going.

A renewed energy fills Krista. In the back seat, Krista sees the girl smile, then nod almost imperceptibly. Yes.

28

Horst looks down at his trembling hands, dry and scratched. He has just finished another button-down shirt and is now hemming a pair of pants, which were tossed carelessly his way by a lieutenant of the current division that is visiting. No "please", "thank you", or "will you", unlike in his shop, where they curry favor from him as a respected tailor. Now, it is just a simple toss as if he were a lowly servant.

Unlike the handsome furnishings and decor of his shop, the room he finds himself in is not in any way "handsome". It is a run-down cabin made of rough wood, one dirty window facing out into the barracks courtyard hastily cemented with a Nazi flag in the middle, and one window, a larger affair, facing out into the woods. The next room holds a toilet, a shower, and an iron utility bed with a thin, moth-eaten mattress. A small window is above a small dresser where Horst keeps his personal effects. Several yards from the window, sheep and some cows can be seen.

Horst reminds himself it is not a prison and gives him comforts others in exile would not have.

The installation houses the mechanics, the tanks they service, and the gunnery, which has its complement of rowdy men who make sure the ammunition and rifles are ready. Thrust into this are two cooks, who boil everything they cook – and him, the only tailor.

Horst reaches for the bag balm in a gray tin. It is his latest acquisition from the farm, stolen in the dead of night from one of the outlying barns where he found it. It is made of lanolin from the farmer's sheep, a product the farmer sells to the SS and their families. He lathers some on sparingly. The balm helps his tired hands, overused from sewing, from bleeding and a creeping arthritis that took the fluidity of movement from his hands.

As Horst marvels at the consistency of the balm and the soothing feel of it, he wishes he were able to find some fruit and even some potatoes, but the stress itself almost wore him out. Horst never had to steal anything in his life until last night. He knew it wouldn't be his last trip, as he needs to familiarize himself with his surroundings to plan to search for his family. Then he knows he won't last unless he has plenty of food and water for what he is about to do.

Soon after his exile to the installation, he tried befriending the farmer, an old-timer who stuck fast to old ways and rules. He could tell the man was not going to risk his life or his sons by even sharing a piece of fruit, when one day Horst "wandered" onto the property to check out his surroundings, including a means of escape. The man appeared suspicious, asked a lot of questions, and short of aiming a rifle at Horst, kept his smile close to his chest. Or so it seemed. These days, Horst is suspicious of everyone, as much as he needs them to be on his side. It appears that he is not the only one who is suspicious.

Horst grapples with his loneliness and never-ending apprehensions about his family by keeping to a strict deadline. He has endless sleepless nights, which creep on him despite his exhaustion from the ten-hour days with only two meals. He feels fortunate for having his privacy, a warm bed, and two meals when he knows word has it from several soldiers that those in forced labor for the worst "crimes" of impurity are subjected to the daily nightmare of slow death by starvation. This afternoon, as the sun descends from its torpor and through the darkness of a foreboding cloud, Horst plots.

By sundown, after quickly eating a meal of warm boiled potatoes and horse meat, Horst spots a building, a house, actually, not much larger than the cabin he is in. He ignored it all this time as he made a mental note to avoid any detection by not making eye contact with any member of rank, such as the lieutenant who rudely tossed a shirt to be hemmed his way. This house seems to be of some importance, as the visiting soldiers of rank seem to frequent it when they are there.

Eleven p.m. strikes, according to the clock on his small nightstand. Horst has kept his work clothes on, still with tendrils of thread clinging to them, and with resolve plops his tired feet into his only boots. He was allowed to keep a few shoes from the home's closet, which were very new.

One was a pair of handsomely stitched dress shoes, which he now has little use for on this perilous journey. Taking in the softness of the Italian leather, Horst proceeds silently toward the bedroom door and then out the front, which was hidden from view by trees lining one part of the courtyard.

The building is a three-story affair, owing to an attic. On this night, there is a spotlight shining towards the courtyard, issuing from an alcove above the building. Horst approaches on an angle, on the side, avoiding the spotlight.

He trips.

Horst's breath is taken out of him as he lands solidly on his chest, his face inhaling the grass. He almost curses out loud, but purses his lips as he quickly sits up and surveys the area.

Silence. He hears the faint laughter of some of the mechanics at the other end of the installation where they are housed in barracks. He darts a look at the gunnery area, where a solitary light from a dorm room lamp betrays a sole man reading. The man didn't even flinch.

Horst scurries to the side of the building, finding purchase on the handle of a door that appears recessed on the side. He turns the rusty knob, and it gives. He peers in and discovers a row of a few steel office desks, utilitarian swivel chairs in old leather – and a bank of filing cabinets. Surely, they would be locked, but he wonders what they house.

Then a cough.

Horst pulls the door shut gently. He surveys and sees a

shirtless soldier, undoubtedly inebriated, headed for the latrine. He is part of the company that came to gather a few tanks. Horst pulls himself as close as possible to the wall as the man slithers unsteadily past.

Then a glimmer as the man's eyes make contact with Horst. "Um, do you have a latrine in here?"

Horst reels back in surprise.

The man is pointing a shaky finger at the door that he just shut.

"No, sorry… It's over there."

The man looks and follows Horst's finger, grins an impish grin, and chuckles. "Yeah, sorry. You are right!"

The man strides off unsteadily, still chuckling.

Horst strides toward his cabin, feeling a need to use the toilet himself, for now giving up. Too many people, too many chances of being questioned.

He enters, breathing and perspiring heavily, shutting the door behind him.

29

Krista blows out her fourteen candles, almost in tears. The cake is beautiful and large, decorated with green buttercream frosting in the shape of a network of ivy. Nestled in the middle is one orange rose surrounded by light pink daisies.

All but one of her pupils, the youngest now eleven years old, attend her birthday party. Frau Dieterstrasse, portly as ever, claps her chubby hands and doles out gold-gilded plates while her twenty-one-year-old son hands out gold forks and embossed napkins with the swastika embroidered on them.

Krista instinctively feels in her pocket a slip of paper as she breathes in and out to calm herself to keep up the farce. She smiles for the benefit of the group and convinces them she is happy. She has, after all, won a citation for being one of the best teachers in the Nazi Youth Corps, and that pleased the Frau immensely, who pulled her into her buxom breast, perfumed with L'Air du Temps after the Nina Ricci factory was raided.

Food of all kinds is passed around. Cheeses from France, Spain and even wine from Portugal. Verde Vinho, she reads on the label as she drinks from a goblet with pieces of lemon and pear. For the first time, the Frau allows her to sit across from her at the head of the table. Fourteen pupils, one out on leave due to illness. Walter. Walter is now twelve and gangly. He looks at her sideways like he did the day he laughed at the labor camp prisoners they saw on a trip to the forest. How he laughed when he saw one of the women fall to her death from a gunshot wound.

Krista pries her mind from the thought, keeping her plastic smile as she eats. She opens her palm under the table and looks at Mila's photograph, smiling back at her, dressed for Krista's birthday. The Frau gave her the photograph that betrayed her parents as if to rub in what led to their arrest. The cruelty of this simple act is not lost on Krista, but she got even by actually thanking the Frau for allowing her to keep it. Krista lovingly keeps it near her. She and Mila stood side by side, companionably holding hands in the living area, as Horst snapped a photo with the new camera.

Then Krista is transported again to their old home in Bleichenbach: the wisteria that crept around the front of the house and the slant of the sun on the kitchen table replete with pink peonies arranged in a glass jar, while her mother removed pits from cherries for borscht. Krista's sunny smile earns her a resolute hug from one of her students, who then stands up from the table to raise a glass of sherry in thanks to their young teacher.

This time, Krista's smile is genuine. Under the table, she tucks the photo into her pocket and resumes eating her birthday cake.

30

Horst grabs the two loaves off the bread cart. What a piece of luck. The farmer just arrived from the adjacent field, his sons in tow in two other trucks. They bring fresh vegetables, fruits and bread the farmer's wife baked, normally depleted by the camp soldiers, but the farmer took this treasure trove to the mechanics and Horst first on this cold morning. Horst learned from one of the mechanics that his group plus the artillery personnel had made a request to reroute. Logistics. The farm is, after all, right next door, so to speak. The Reich is willing to please their support staff, as it means functioning tanks ready for battle and much-needed ammunition.

Not one human in the group questions Horst, as the few SS men stationed there are away at a major meeting. One of those meetings where important updates are discussed, which means a head count of how many dead and how many civilians have been deported.

Horst eagerly pockets nectarines, pears and the strawberries from the greenhouses, thinking of how he can preserve them for the walk through the forest. It is only early April, so there is still a chill in the air. He decides the strawberries won't last unless they were preserved. He eats them on the way back to his cabin, caught in reverie: He thinks of his daughter's birthday that month.

Horst enters his rustic and humble quarters: the shop itself with the one large table, two small ones by the window, which hold the sewing machines he was given to work with, and mannequins standing at attention, all with uniforms in stages of being sewn. He was given ten-hour days with a brief lunch with the mechanics at the next mess room, where he learned how valuable they all were to the Reich. He feels fortunate to be alive as long as he is needed.

Horst walks past the large table with the cloth pieces for the makings of another uniform, tattered remains of sewing tape, all sorts of patterns, and the detritus of a tailor's shop. He has to keep working as he plans his exodus from the installation. He swiftly enters his little bedroom and shuts the door.

On the bed, strewn about, are two maps he found behind one of the filing cabinets in the building. He was finally able to enter in the hours of the early morning right after the SS guards left. He sits down on the chair by the dresser, pulling out all the fruits and bread he was able to collect, as thoughts run through his mind of the path he has to take to avoid detection.

He thinks about the file cabinets and how he left them, hoping he didn't forget to replace anything.

The cabinets.

One cabinet held all sorts of equipment requisitions, contracts and miscellaneous items, including the uniforms required and those that were being returned for him to mend, if not bloodied or destroyed. He hated those when they came in, as it was a testament to the violence of war and the inhuman ways of the Nazis, who stripped their own soldiers to reuse the uniforms after death. But that cabinet and the next one didn't concern him. The one near a window did, however.

Horst approached the tall cabinet, painted army green and pockmarked with years of use, and hoped he would find his own personnel file. Surely, there was a way to find out what or how they'd disposed of his little family. Unlike the others, this one was locked. He took out a sewing needle, then another, and began fiddling with the lock. After an hour or so, he detected the red glow of approaching morning from the window above the cabinet and again was about to give up.

Then a glint caught his eye.

Resting on the edge of the cabinet, almost ready to fall to the back, was a key. It was not like a door key, but a short, stubby one.

He reached for it. It fit.

The foraging into the cabinet practically blurred his vision, as he feared what he may find if he did find his file. Tearing up, suppressing a sob, hopelessness and despair almost overtook him. The files were a conglomeration of personnel, which was what he wanted. He had to compose himself. Riffling through each file, he found they were not in alphabetical order; then he realized it was by trade. He looked under the "Miscellaneous" section, as he was the only tailor, and then, finally, found his file was right in front.

"Schneider, Horst Haber."

"Eisenach"

31

KRISTA RIFFLES through the Frau's personal effects, searching for a key to the study next door. She is up on the third floor of the "maison de maitre", an unusual home in German terms, built after French architecture. After being in a simple rental cottage, then an upscale home built by means, she found that the Frau had been appointed a home much larger than the one she thought impressive. This "house" is the size of a small building.

It takes Krista a while, a few weeks after the party, to glean that the Frau knows the disposition of the rest of Krista's family. Listening enrapt from her obscure perch by the conservatory, which connects to the dining room, she overheard from a guest that the child mentors of the Nazi Youth are squirreled away near installations, and this home is in Budingen. She wonders if her father is in the same town, as there is an army camp nearby. She hopes beyond measure that her parents, and even Mila, are all still alive, but also busies herself with the elements of the day, as it is one way to survive. Krista knows that to ask directly means a desire to escape the confines of the regimen of home to school and to her pupils.

Her days never vary, though on weekends, the Frau grants her the chauffeur to shop the city in the company of one of the brownshirts who double as servants in the house. Krista feels prying eyes on her all the time, except when she is in her bedroom. Or, in this case, right after Saturday's lunches, which go on for hours in the large dining room replete with blanche de chine statutes staring at guests from their perches amid chinoiserie.

A dining room that opens onto a stone veranda... and voices that echo into the conservatory.

All the servants are there, either milling in the kitchen at the housekeeper's behest, or in the dining room. Two or three always tend the garden, for the Frau loves her huge garden, always free of weeds. In the garden's center, four stone paths converge to purple wisteria circling a large wooden gazebo.

Krista has earned a modicum of trust from the Frau after her little teaching award and excuses herself from the dining table, where some men of rank are partaking of a luncheon of quails in a bed of chanterelle mushrooms. Amid the culinary feasting, no one approaches her as she ascends the marble steps to her bedroom, then the hallway, down past the quarters of the Frau's twenty-one-year-old son, and up the steps to the Frau's bedroom on the third floor.

Past the library on the right, a sitting room with a large balcony opens to the front of the house. Directly across from the sitting room is the Frau's bedroom suite, which has its own bath. Krista enters the cool room, well away from the prying eyes below. Out of curiosity, she surveys the room and enters the high-ceilinged bathroom in the same color scheme. Everything seems a study in pale yellows and blues. Then a connecting door past the dressing area of the bathroom – which is locked.

Krista looks into the keyhole and surmises from the age of the mansion that it will be a large key. Based on the age of their village home, it will be rusted, large and easy to spot. Then she hears what she thinks is rustling through the door. Someone is in the room. Slowly, Krista backs away, almost hitting a large bureau in the Frau's dressing room, recessed towards the wall and hidden behind the woman's dresses. She looks at the bureau and sees that a man's personal effects are atop the dresser. Shaving items, a man's comb and a man's watch. Idly, Krista wonders if the Frau has a lover, as she knows the husband is away at the front lines. Who is next door?

Krista pulls away from the door quietly and slowly pries open the dresser. What she sees stupefies her.

Inside the bureau, men's clothing and the accoutrements of what appears to be a garter with a rubber penis attached. Then lotions and lubricants, the latter Krista surmises are for the teats of cows when they lactate. It makes her blush. There are no cows for miles. Then the bottom drawer. Krista sees a small album bound in leather. Now avid with curiosity, she opens it. Photograph upon photograph of a nude woman, slimmer and much younger than the Frau, with dark hair, looks back at the camera. As

Krista turns the pages, in several it appears that the Frau is posed nude in a bedroom that is much better draped in satin and brocade than the Frau's next to the adjoining bathroom. Shocked, Krista wonders if the husband, not the Frau has taken a lover and is now with her, which accounts for his absence in the house.

She flips to the next page. Krista's eyes pop out as she sees a photo of the Frau sitting on an ottoman, one hand clutching the younger woman's hand, who is seated side by side with their thighs touching.

They are both nude.

Suddenly, it dawns on Krista who the person may be who is hidden next door. The woman is the Frau's lover.

Then, almost confirming her thoughts, she hears a book page flip near the locked door and a woman clearing her throat.

32

Horst rewraps the sausages from the cook, a large piece of bread, and a wedge of cheese into his messenger bag. A piece of tailor's paper with drawings of clothing and patterns of clothing has been hastily shoved in for good measure should someone ask where he is headed – a tailor on a mission to sell his designs at the next village. Hearing about the Russians who are descending rapidly into Germany didn't help, but his benign demeanor as a humble tailor he hopes will gain him passage.

Horst has befriended the cook and explained during lunch that he will be checking on his wife in the village. Without guards, as it is a low-profile camp for support staff of the regime, the cook didn't even flinch and gave him a few days' rations of meat and even offered the cheese wheel and jam in an entire jar to take as a present to his wife. Horst had to accept all the man's generosity even if the jar bulged in his bag, as Horst doesn't know how long or how far he has to go to locate Krista and their means of escape.

Images of her and Agatha float in his thoughts and propel him to move faster. Any day now the soldiers assigned to the installation will return, grateful for a brief respite from their duties as sentries, watching the ammunition and tanks: The primary, but boring purpose of their job.

Horst now knows Krista is alive and hopefully well as a Nazi Youth teacher. The papers indicated she was "rehomed" with Frau Dieterstrasse to continue her career as a "youth mentor" for the Reich. The woman's husband was assigned behind the front as a colonel and headquartered in Munich, well away from the Frau, who heads and appoints the Youth Corps mentors. He hopes Krista has not been indoctrinated and brainwashed as some of the mechanics' children have been. However, he knows his daughter is great at discerning character, and hopes she did not cave in to the corruptive atmosphere.

Horst measures, cuts and tapes the clothing he is preparing for the next regiment, mindful of the time and the schedule he has. He wants to make sure the cook's story does not arouse suspicion among the soldiers should he be prodded on Horst's hasty departure. Still, he does not want to leave by day nor take a train, which usually has a regiment of soldiers and higher-ranking officers who might identify him. By the time a higher-ranked officer catches the lie, he hopes he would be well on his way and his path undetected. He worries about the cheese, as it is rather ripe, mindful of the shepherd dogs who accompany the search parties of the Gestapo should it come to that. His work suggests he is meeting all the requests for clothing and uniforms on time, so he languishes in that success, as he hopes it will lend further credence to his "brief" departure.

Horst decides he will wash whatever he leaves behind prior to leaving to minimize his scent should a dog search ensue. His bedclothes he now covers in lime, as the soldiers do with the cadavers of the dead that they throw or shoot in ditches. Horst prays he will not see what happened to Agatha, as he knows she has been sent to a camp, which the papers did not elaborate upon. Night upon night, as Horst lay in bed, he awakes to night terrors of his wife being subjected to what he has heard the Nazis do in experiments. Paralyzed, he watches her, helpless as he kneels, praying that it is all just that. A nightmare.

With the stealth of a cat on to its nighttime prowl, Horst exits the cabin that has been his home for over a year. As he heads for the adjacent pasture, he realizes his daughter's fourteenth birthday has already passed. Dimly, he thinks of the depravity of war, which not only takes away life, but the vicissitudes that herald loss and hardship. It makes him angry and gives him renewed vigor to trod through the field with determination in his stride, the abundant food in his bag reminding him he will not, for the moment, starve.

As he strides forward, mindful of snakes and the possibility of mines, he observes tendrils of smoke several miles away. Gray smoke unlike that of firewood. It comes with a scent he is at a loss to define.

He moves on.

33

KRISTA OPENS the bathroom door and almost runs into the Frau's ample bosom. The scent of L'Air du Temps assails her and almost makes her turn back if not for the Frau's restraining hand gripping her sleeve.

"Why are you here?!"

Veins are pronounced on the woman's fat cheeks, her face a shade of pink, which contrasts to her heavy frame draped in a yellow dress suitable for the luncheon she is hosting below.

"I was just looking around and curious, I guess." Krista's explanation, quickly done in a decision to remain calm and matter-of-fact, softens the woman's demeanor.

"These are my private apartments. Private."

"I'm sorry for the intrusion."

Frau Dieterstrasse examines Krista's face, trying to elucidate a motive.

Krista makes a move to leave, and the Frau puts a hand up.

"I will give you a tour. After all, you're living here, and you're one of my best mentors."

Krista smiles the smile of one who appears honored.

"But there's nothing to see in my bathroom. Come, follow me."

Krista gives a smile, now curious what the Frau is willing to reveal.

She quickly hides inside the left pocket of her blue party dress the photo of the Frau with the dark-haired woman sitting close together, naked.

With a perfunctory tone, the Frau spreads her hands to show how she has decorated the bath. "You see, I always loved wisteria... Are you familiar with plants?"

Krista places one finger on her chin, as if thinking as she again surveys the wallpaper with embossed wisteria vines, which snake their way towards the high ceiling. "When I see wisteria, I think of my mama."

The Frau pauses, looking back at Krista as if she has been slapped. Her tone is incongruous with her reply. "I am sorry you do. Perhaps we should go to my bedroom – it has a nice leafy pattern."

Krista turns to the bedroom and walks out of the bathroom, surveying the window curtains tied back with gold tassels. "Everything reminds me of her."

The Frau stops, frowning. "It's not my goal to make you homesick for things that are now permanently in the past. Move on, you must."

The last sentence is like a reprimand, a slap.

"Wouldn't you miss your mother if you had one?"

"Of course. My mother..." The Frau stops. "Let's go back to the drawing room."

The Frau turns to leave.

"I'd like to know what happened to my mother."

The Frau turns back, facing Krista head-on. "Do you really want to know? Really?"

The woman's expression, hard, cold, tells Krista everything she dreads to hear. Her mother is dead. Gone. Torn from her life. That tone told her what she dreaded.

Krista swallows. "How about my father?"

The Frau softens. It is clear he has been dealt a softer blow. "He remains a tailor where he can help the Reich."

A feminine cough, now more pronounced, issues from the next room. Quickly, the Frau approaches the bathroom door, shutting it.

Krista seizes the opportunity. "Who is that?"

"One of the maids – my valet."

"She takes all her meals here?"

The Frau gives Krista a stabbing look.

"She sounds sick."

Krista makes for the bathroom, opening the door, rushing in and grabbing the knob to the dressing room's connecting door, where the young woman's coughs can clearly be heard.

The Frau grabs Krista's arm. "YOU are NOT to go there!"

"Tell me where my father is!"

The Frau turns Krista's shoulders with her hands, pinning the girl against the dressing room wall. "Why? After I took you in and showed you..."

"Tell me where my father is."

"No."

Krista turns the knob. The Frau slaps her hand.

Krista reveals the photograph in her pocket, holding it with both hands. "Is this the girl next door?"

The Frau's face blanches. She appears about to faint.

The Frau tries to grab the photograph.

Karma, Krista thinks. *I'll use the photo the same way my parents were arrested.*

"Tell me where my father is, and I won't tell anyone about you and her." Krista's lips point to the door beyond.

A feminine voice issues from behind the door. "Maillie? What's the matter?"

The Frau pauses. With resignation, she reluctantly opens the adjoining door, revealing a young woman in her early thirties. The same one in the photograph. She is more beautiful than the picture.

"Krista, meet Adelie. Adelie, my best teacher."

The young woman unbends from the settee, gracefully approaching Krista. She touches Krista's face tenderly. Scars line the woman's wrists.

Adelie speaks. "Tell her where her father is like you told me where mine was... in Buchenwald."

34

Horst stumbles, almost landing on one knee. Ahead, a deep wood in the twilight. He looks behind him – no farmhouse, just a forest. He is now completely engulfed by the wood. Horst has been walking briskly for about three hours, his thirst becoming more and more pronounced.

He glances at his watch, which shows 10:15 p.m. Another gift from Brigadefuhrer Beyer that he chose not to confiscate. He spots a tree limb, sturdy, leafless. He grabs it from the forest floor to use as a walking stick, eyes a boulder in a clearing, and heads for it. Wearily, he sits, unraveling the messenger bag from his shoulder.

A twig snaps.

Horst swivels to look behind him, alarmed.

A doe stands motionless, eyes reflecting back, studying him.

Horst exhales in relief.

From the bag, he pulls out a bottle of water still glistening from condensation. He takes a swig, inhales again.

He closes his eyes, dreaming.

He hears a young woman singing.

Horst's eyes open in disbelief.

The sound stops.

Surely, he was dreaming, even delirious.

He reopens the bag and reluctantly reveals the loaf of bread from the cook. Horst rewrapped it in a light blue handkerchief. He breaks off a small piece, places it on the boulder, reaching in for the wheel of cheese and a knife, which he hid in a pocket of the bag.

He slices, hungrily chewing the cheese and bread. He decides he will chew them at least twenty times, though he does not succeed, so famished is he from the combined effort of escape, fear of detection, and a hike he is unaccustomed to. He slices more bread, cuts another piece of cheese, looking around him for anyone who might be walking.

The singing, a lullaby, resumes.

A girl's voice, strangely familiar, which is lost on Horst at the moment.

His face registers a growing familiarity, curiosity and wonderment at the voice he hears.

He stands, the embroidered handkerchief falling from his lap as he attempts to locate the sound.

Suddenly, the wind blows; the singing stops.

Quickly, Horst packs away the food, closing the bag with haste and swinging it back on his shoulder. He looks up at a ridge to his left and scampers up with renewed energy.

Behind him, the blue cloth lies on the ground.

A gale-force wind blows again; this time the handkerchief sails in the air and is taken up flying.

As the handkerchief lands, a pink peony is evidently embroidered on it.

35

CRICKETS SING. Krista steps out onto the patio, a small covered basket in one hand, a canvas rucksack secured by straps to her back. Wrapped in a spring coat, wearing boots and a green flowered dress she found new at the previous house, she looks up at the Frau's bedroom window. The Frau watches her and gives one wave, a sad look on the woman's face. At another window, she sees the slim face of Adelie smiling.

Krista steps off the patio and swiftly walks the expanse of lawn that joins the narrow road towards the town. She told both women she would catch a train to Eisenach, over one hundred miles north, where her father is stationed. She hopes they believed her, as she has no intention of using the trains for fear of apprehension should they be persuaded to give her away.

In her rucksack, the Frau told her to pack a spare Youth Corps uniform should she need it. It might come of use, the Frau said, depending on whom she encountered. For now, she is a regular German girl, blonde and blue-eyed, walking through the forest in search of truffles – and getting lost.

Krista clutches a map given to her by the Frau, who reluctantly cooperated to let her go in exchange for Krista's silence about her relationship with Adelie. It was not lost on Krista that the Frau had fallen in love with a Jew and another woman at that.

Krista crosses the road, minding any traffic that may be passing, and enters the woods beyond. It is just another late spring day that a Youth Corps teacher is defecting to search for her exiled father and mother, she thinks cynically.

Pitch is the color that awaits her. Krista trudges on, but has to pause as the woods deepen. Glancing behind her, she notes the receding light from the road, which is only brightened by the sky above. Here, shrouded in complete darkness by the canopy of deepening wood, she has to readjust her eyes.

Krista shuts her eyes and then opens them again, blinking. She surveys the terrain, the branches on the ground, the kudzu, the thick canopy of maples, birch, walnut and ferns that grow to cover the forest floor. A chorus of frogs and all manner of animals preparing to rest for the night covers her ears.

Then, amidst the natural sounds of night, she hears the faint sounds of a vehicle, like a truck, approaching the road.

Krista tightly clutches the strap of the canvas rucksack secured to her back and the woven basket – filled with all manner of food from the Frau. She darts quickly through the brush, disappearing in the thicket as an army truck trolls by, a Nazi flag flying. She wishes her mother, even her father, were here with her to explain why Hitler turned their lives upside down.

Her mother had an explanation for everything.

36

A DETAILED WORN map is spread out on a boulder; a small lantern nearby sits stretching tendrils of light in the gloaming. Horst's finger traces a path through a large forest on the map, stretching almost from Eisenach down to Budingen, just north of Frankfurt. There is no path, only a wooded expanse that he can see.

The forest sounds around him lull him to an almost fever pitch of slumber. His eyes are almost closing with exhaustion. Suddenly, a silence.

The forest is dead.

Gunshots.

Horst's eyes open wide. In the eerie silence, he heard what he perceived as gunshots. Quickly, he refolds the map, stuffs it into his bag, and reshoulders it. Gazing at the lantern, he shuts it off, plummeting the wood into darkness.

Something compels him to look down at his vest, a thin

quilted affair he sewed himself for chilly evenings when he sewed late. A dark spot is widening, soaking the buttons and the quilt. He touches it and smells blood, aghast.

Seated on the boulder and his bag shouldered on him, he stands, disoriented by the blood. Has he just been shot?

He feels no different. In fact, he just feels as he did before, save for the fatigue of the hike.

He unshoulders the bag, begins unbuttoning his vest in fear, checking his body for injuries.

Unbuttoning his shirt, he discovers no source of the blood. The blood is confined to his clothing, which appears in his hands, now loose and apart from him, to keep widening with blood. The shirt and vest are eventually soaked.

More gunshots.

Without spare clothing, Horst keeps examining the bloody clothes, totally perplexed. He cannot risk turning the lamp back on for fear of giving away his position. Not even his small flashlight. Dashing away from his spot in the clearing, he examines the ground for blood, but can't tell in the darkness. He intended to doze off before walking again, but he needs to locate the origin of the sounds. Perhaps a hunter has shot game, and it fell near him, accounting for the blood. He looks up at the ridge near him and decides that what may be happening can safely be viewed from above.

Horst seeks purchase, reaching for branches and roots as he clambers up, hoping no one will detect the scent of the blood on the clothes or himself. It is what he fears the most if the Nazis were in pursuit. Leaving the clothing is nonsense. He needs protection from the elements. He will find a stream to wash it off, whatever it is, as soon as he deems it is safe and there is some light.

Still perplexed, he struggles towards the last few feet of the small ridge, grabbing a tree limb and finally falling into a seated position.

Below Horst, he sees what appears to be a dim bluish light. Several yards from his position, he watches as several soldiers appear to be in a line facing several people who are facing them.

Then more shots.

Like marionettes without strings, the people fall.

Horst smells the overpowering scent of gunpowder.

Then one soldier wallows away like a drunken man, away from the line.

And towards Horst.

He drops his rifle.

Grabs a pistol hidden in his boot.

The man, spindly with youth, clambers drunkenly up towards the ridge. Horst hides behind the tree, breathing hard.

The man reaches the top, just a few feet from Horst.

He aims his pistol to his chin.

And fires.

Blood jettisons from the man's head, spreading flesh and brain matter all over the tree branches above Horst.

Horst hears his own screams.

Eyes wide, he crawls away, unable to stand in disbelief.

Then silence.

Horst finally stands, sweeping off the entrails from his

body. He trips as he attempts to walk away and rolls back down the embankment, his momentum finally stopped by the lantern he left behind and his heavy bag.

He cries, emotionally exhausted, and falls into an uneasy slumber.

37

A SHADOW BLOCKS Krista's view of the sun streaming through the leaves above her. Blinking, she attempts to discern the figure above her and is instantly gripped with fear. She sits up, her dress wet from the morning dew. Water drips from the leaves that shielded her from the night's weather.

She looks around, stiff from her sleeping position, and turns in time to see –

A woman with a worn and simple dress, walking away – the profile of a familiar face turns toward Krista – then it is gone.

Agatha, her mother.

"Mama!"

Krista stands up in the early stillness of morning, her movement stirring a cacophony of birds. She darts towards the meadow where the woman was headed, and looks around.

"Mama?!"

A breeze blows.

A pause.

A deep stillness.

Here and there, Krista dashes around the thicket of wildness, her legs bending and tangling within the undisturbed understory.

Krista looks back at her rucksack and basket still where she left them. She wants to surge forward to locate the woman, but feels conflicted about leaving her map and belongings, which she so needs in order to move on.

Finally, hunger takes over and wins. Krista walks back, sits, digging for breakfast, the first meal since she began her walk two days ago.

She spots her bottle of water, now half empty.

As she eats a peach, she surveys the area, hoping her mother is somewhere in the woods, looking for her and the rest. She felt the deep stirrings of hunger, more instinctive, but now assuaged, she again longs for a familiar and comforting face.

Charged with renewed energy, Krista gathers her belongings and again darts towards the meadow where she saw the figure of Agatha. She can't comprehend why her mother didn't reply when she called to her, visible as she thought her to be. She wonders if it was wishful thinking and perhaps a hallucination brought on by hunger and her desire.

38

DEAD LEAVES BLOW onto Horst's face, awakening him. He sits up, hearing a rustle behind him.

A dog. Scraggly, thin, fur around its eyes turned white. An old German shepherd.

The shepherd paused from its digging, one paw still up, observing Horst. In the process of digging, the leaves were strewn in Horst's direction.

Man and dog stare entranced at each other. An unexpected introduction. Then it dawns on Horst the events of the previous night: The soldier who shot himself after shooting a line of civilian prisoners.

Horst looks up the ridge behind him, the dog still paused in observation.

Horst looks down at himself, feeling disgust as he recalls the man's flesh and brains spewing forth. Arterial blood had jetted on him.

But there is nothing on him but his own sweat, dirt and mud.

Surprised, Horst continues to examine himself as the dog sits, almost as riveted as he.

He stands up. He examines his shirt –

his pants –

and his own hair.

Other than the leaves and dirt the dog strewed on top of him while he slept, no evidence of any human violence.

The young soldier, who appeared about sixteen years of age, only stood a few feet from Horst.

Horst should have been covered in blood, brain matter and perhaps even pieces of the dead man's hair.

Thoughts and a panoply of amazement floods Horst as he wonders whether his fear-immersed and thirsty brain is causing him to see things.

Then the dog approaches. Horst quickly and protectively grabs his messenger bag, which contains the food.

The dog has something within its jaws.

The dog drops it.

A long bone, gristle still attached, plops onto the leaf-covered ground.

The dog sits, its tail wagging, as if awaiting recognition of its gift.

Horst examines and nudges the bone with his foot. The dog whines, looking at him and back at the bone. An offering. Horst, interpreting the dog's gesture as want, digs in his bag and produces a piece of cheese, cutting it and tossing it towards the dog.

Hungrily, the dog wolfs down the cheese, smiling a dog smile, panting.

A breeze blows, wafting with it a sickeningly sweet

scent. The moment of morbidity sinks in with it, and Horst's brain registers death once again. There is death nearby. He looks up at the ridge, feeling repelled, sickened and almost on the verge of vomiting.

But he doesn't.

Instead, Horst grabs the bone, turns the object in his hands, squinting at the dog, which looks back, head tilted.

Then, as he examines both bone and dog, the hair on his head begins to prickle. He glances at the dog, gazes back at the bone and stares at the animal's hindquarters.

The dog has presented him with a dog's hindquarters.

Horst spots a skull right behind the shepherd. Slowly, he drops the bone and stands, approaching the skull with trepidation, but his curiosity wins out.

A dog's skull.

Horst straightens, surveying the field adjacent to the ridge. More bones.

A sweet scent assails him again as he moves closer and realizes he has stumbled onto a field of animal bones.

Horst looks back at the German shepherd.

The poor dog, almost skin and bones, looks starved. Horst puts two and two together as the animal darts away and rummages among the recent carcasses further afield, eating what remains of his comrades.

The dog, desperate to feed, has become a cannibal.

This time, Horst throws up his meal.

Filled with unease, Horst reluctantly looks up at the ridge where he rolled off in his haste to get away from the suicide last night. Feeling a need to check what might lie above the ridge, Horst ascends again with dread.

At the ridge's summit, Horst sees the now familiar landscape – but there is nothing but a meadow.

Then, ahead, the river stretches for several yards where he saw a line of civilians shot dead one by one in a line facing a line of German soldiers.

Horst breathes in, still grappling with the previous night's violent nightmare, still taking in the enormity of the slaughter and the young soldier's culminating act of self-destruction.

He bows with the weight of it, emotional and physical exhaustion bending him like an old man as he places his hands on his knees for support.

Horst bends the branches out of the way and emerges onto the meadow to inspect and make sense of what he witnessed the previous night.

By Horst's feet, he spots a glinting piece of metal.

A Nazi pin encrusted with blood.

Horst tentatively reaches for it, holding it in his hands. A confirmation that he was not hallucinating.

Behind Horst, the shepherd whines.

39

Krista reties her boots, now crusty and worn. The soles are still intact, but she yearns to remove them and soak them in a stream, a river, or any body of water. She glances at her bottle of water. Empty. She also needs a bath, having already changed into her uniform days ago when she attempted to wash with what little water she had left. Judging from the mud on the edges of her uniform skirt, a Nazi-issue khaki, now turned brown with dirt, miles of traversing the wood show on her. Specks of green slime dot her white shirt. She removed her beige tie and secured it around her head to ward off the sweat from her eyes. She surely is a mess. Not used to weeks of being unwashed, she cringes and itches with discomfort. Krista thinks about pulling out her dress, which she stuffed into the pack after changing into cleaner clothing. Now, both are filthy.

Furthermore, her lips are chapped. She knows it was a matter of time before her thirst led to dehydration. Krista stands, munching hungrily on the last of her apple. Its juice temporarily quenches her thirst.

She opens a cloth napkin – one sausage left.

A rooster crows somewhere in the distance. Krista darts towards the source of the crowing. Between a copse of large walnuts and maple, Krista peers. Ahead in the distance, she spots what appears to be a bunch of straws. Too regular to be part of the natural landscape.

Perplexed, she emerges, now walking with determination to determine what she is seeing. She is up on a hill where trees obscure part of her view. She is looking down at bales of hay.

And there are more.

She parts the branches and steps out close to the crest.

Rolls of hay punctuate the landscape dotted by cows busily chewing.

On one side stands a sprawling stone farmhouse, shutters open to the sun. Then two barns appear as she continues to ascend. A pasture with a field of sheep. Goats. A shed facing where she is standing closest, the view obstructed now by another group of trees, the lip of the hill. It seems she was on a low ridge.

A rooster emerges, pecking. It must be the rooster she heard.

Krista has visions of eggs, perhaps even some fruit. As if on command, a young girl whose hair and gait resemble Mila emerges from within the shed, tossing feed from a basket. Hens roam and peck. Again, as if encouraging Krista, hens cackle as more feed scatters on the dry ground.

Hungrily, Krista eyes the hens.

Then the girl looks up in Krista's direction, blonde bangs obscuring her eyes.

Mila?

Eyes round with amazement, Krista almost calls out to the girl. Krista ducks, not ready to reveal herself. She wishes her mother were here to explain what she is seeing. A pang of grief intermingled with loneliness grips Krista.

The girl turns and darts towards another building. Another shed, larger than the first. This one is encircled by ground cobbled with pebbles. A courtyard of sorts with a water pump and an inviting spigot. Water drips from it, spreading and glinting on the pebbles in the morning sun. Beyond it, a thin road snakes to the woods beyond.

Krista now hears a pail being moved – the bottom scraping the ground. The girl has positioned a rusted pail under the spigot, and water sloshes as the girl pumps. The girl has her back turned to her as she pumps.

Fresh water. It is more than Krista can bear.

Thirst and curiosity propel Krista to stand, risking revealing her presence. She surveys the beamed farmhouse for movement. The windows are curtained in a veil resembling lace. It spurs a memory of her mother's embroidered curtains.

Her rucksack on her back, she approaches, the view now yielding all of the smaller sheds and the sounds of the hens as they cackle, mocking. Right beneath her, just a few yards off.

She descends towards the farm.

40

Running as fast as the tall grass allows him, Horst flies. He heard an approaching truck, then men talking, laughing as if life were a picnic. He needs to put distance between himself and the passing convoy, which means getting past the river, where the bodies could still be floating. Horst keeps his eyes averted, focused on the shepherd, which darts ahead.

Horst is at a loss. In his own mind, he can't rationalize what happened last night; the soldier shooting himself just within a few feet of Horst, spewing brain matter and pieces of skull on him, his clothing and all around them.

Horst recalls vividly hearing, smelling and seeing in detail the young soldier's anguished face and the ensuing self-inflicted violence he meted on himself and Horst's psyche. It was just moments after an entire line of townspeople were shot by a squad of soldiers, of which the young man was one.

Now, in the light of day, it is as if it were just a nightmare.

Except for the swastika pin stained with dry blood.

How did Horst come away so clean? To add to the tragedy, he had come upon a dog, obviously a shepherd of the Reich, starving and so hungry that it ate its neglected comrades. Those remains and bones make sense to Horst.

As Horst goes past the field where he saw the animal carcasses of the shepherds, he searches for evidence of the human massacre with dread. Several yards further, he finally encounters evidence: Pieces of clothing near the river.

As he approaches with one arm covering his nose in expectation of the sweet scent of death, he sees what may be the skeletal frames within the clothing. All in a line they are, with berets and hats near what would have been old men; scarves and lace and flowered clothing of women and children. Small clothing around small bones. Children. BUT the bodies have been picked clean and are bones. Finally his arm comes down, as there is no scent of death. How can a gruesome scene that he witnessed last night become bones by morning? By morning. They are all bones. Impossible.

Floating in the river's debris are all manner of possessions: hat boxes; luggage; what was once an open parasol beautiful in its flowered pattern floats by, soiled with mud. It was obvious they've been there for at least a year, maybe two judging from how the textiles are bleached of their color. As a tailor, Horst knows how long it takes for fabrics to fade. Horst can't bear to look anymore. Then the instinct to survive overtakes him and thoughts of where he will need to get clean, uncontaminated water. He glances down at the bottle in his one hand, almost empty.

Then the dog. It is waiting for him, it seems, at the edge of the other side of what appears to be a stream, soaking wet. Horst pauses as the trucks' engines fade in the distance, alone again with the remains of human cruelty.

Stoically, Horst braves the thinnest part of the river, strewn with boulders and rocks for him to cross. One foot ahead of the other, he crosses in small steps, minding his weak ankles from spraining, or worse, breaking on the molding boulders.

Once in a while he thinks he sees pieces of torn clothing and human detritus float by.

Focus.

Don't look.

Solid ground.

Then he crosses the stream.

The dog waits, then wanders off as soon as Horst makes it across.

"Wait!"

The shepherd pauses and turns.

Horst has a new companion.

41

Into the ramshackle shed, Krista squirrels herself, looking around at her new surroundings. From her new position, Krista can hear the girl working the pump. Krista surveys the shed: It is used for storage. All manner of farming tools hang from the sides, where light shows through the slats, and she can see the girl outside.

Krista picks her way across the cluttered ground strewn with hay, soil and tools, mindful of hitting anything that would give her away. She makes it to one of the walls clear of tools where a bale of hay sits. She decides she will hide there and perhaps spend the night until she can further observe who they are and if they are pro- or anti-Reich like her family. If they are pro-Nazi, her uniform may help, but then they'd ask why she is alone and dirty. If they are against it, then she has to change to the dress before she is discovered. She is eager to determine where food is cached and, more importantly, who the girl is. She looks so much like Mila that Krista's heart aches.

Krista hopes so.

With great thirst, Krista avidly watches the pail of water, the girls' back turned to her. She is filling a wooden trough.

Then the girl tugs at the heavy object now sloshing with water.

Why not pull it first towards the hens before filling it?

Krista puts two and two together, now very curious about the girl. The girl is obviously challenged in some way.

Her heart goes out to her, wishing she could help, and then Krista sees the girl push the trough, toppling it.

Precious water spills from the vessel, leaching its way between the cobblestones. She is so thirsty she can feel the water go down her throat.

Then the sound of a motor from the adjacent field.

A thresher.

A woman calls out from the now open farmhouse door.

The girl looks up.

Frustrated by the motor's noise, Krista can't make out the name. The girl is obviously being summoned.

The girl darts away towards the farmhouse in response.

They have to be pro-Reich. How else could they be out here as if nothing is happening in the world around them. She wishes her mother were with her to explain. She always had an answer. Krista eyes the pail and the trough. She reluctantly shoulders her pack and places her basket behind the bale of hay. Determinedly she makes her way towards the shed door.

She exits, making her way while darting glances at the farmhouse in the distance.

A few more yards to the water spout.

Outside, she leans against the shed's wall, inching her way toward the cobbled area. Hens emerge from the adjacent shed – the henhouse.

The hens cluck.

Two hens look up and trot away.

A few more steps.

Slowly she eyes the farmhouse.

No one.

The door remains closed.

Krista approaches now, feeling the slippery and smooth stones beneath the threadbare soles of her boots.

A foot away. She can smell the water.

Krista reaches for the water handle and bears down.

Water gushes onto the stones.

Krista eagerly places her lips near the spigot, drinks as she bears down on the water handle.

Like a starved animal she hears herself sucking noisily as she assuages her thirst.

Nearby, the upturned trough. She glances up at the still farmhouse. She takes the bucket, fills it, and pushes the trough towards the henhouse. She fills it from the bucket.

Then a peck on her head.

Krista turns to discover a hen, inches from her head.

She returns to drink and then reaches for the bucket, refilling it to wash her arms and then her legs.

Relief floods her features.

The hen trots around and then disappear into the henhouse. Others follow.

Krista watches.

She follows and enters.

Eggs lie cradled in hay.

Krista quickly surveys the area. She's alone and starving. She spots a rusted wire basket nearby, designed with a fleur-de-lis. Hens roost by a crate, clucking noisily at her intrusion.

She reaches for the basket and begins tucking in the eggs, oblivious to the hens clucking in anger. The shells are still soft, just hours from being laid. A hen pecks at her hand, then another.

Krista pulls away, then shoos the hen. It takes flight, and the rest follow, showering Krista with feathers and dust motes. As the feathers settle, she sees a wooden crate. A makeshift table she can use, if she can just find a way to cook the eggs. She looks in.

There, amidst the feathers and chicken droppings, lies a blue handkerchief with an embroidery of a pink peony.

Krista grabs the handkerchief and, in her exuberance, suddenly sits. The scent of her mother's perfume lingers on it. She inhales it as a flood of memories signaling a longing for reunion assails her internal vision of her mother's kitchen.

She looks around, now alive, joyous and hopeful. Her mother or someone from her family was here. Or IS here.

In the distance, a door creaks open.

42

Exhausted, hurting, cold and hungry, Horst finally surrenders to his body and sits on a boulder.

"Come."

The shepherd pauses and turns back, stopping and sitting beside Horst. Tail wagging, the dog eagerly watches Horst dig into his bag. The wedge of cheese, now just a few bites left, is all he has besides a few sausages. The dog looks away and sniffs, his nose pointing downhill.

In the growing twilight, Horst stands and spots the dog approaching a small stream. This looks clear, unlike the one he previously crossed hours ago. Horst approaches, seeing rocks and pebbles at the bottom of the clear water.

Hungrily, he dips the water bottle, filling it. Then schools of small fish evade his hand. More fish pass.

Sardines, Horst thinks as his stomach yields to hunger.

The dog approaches, a branch in its mouth. Horst pauses, taken aback by the intelligence of his companion. He takes it, patting the dog on the head. He pulls out a small knife and starts to whittle the branch, making a spear.

In the distance, the shrill sound of a whistling train disrupts Horst's concentration. Beyond the impending darkness within the trees, he spots what appears to be a train trestle several miles off.

He decides he will explore the possibility of riding the train south. Quickly, Horst stands and is determined to have a meal for both of them. He spears at the stream, water spewing as he aims and hits at one fish and another.

Hours pass. The darkness deepens as it descends from twilight to night. Horst walks away from the stream, tossing the homemade spear in disgust to the ground in frustration. He grabs his water jug and returns to the water's edge, leans over, refilling it. He's all sweaty now. He looks up at the fading light, and the train trestle is no longer visible. In resignation, he sips his water, then pours it over his head. He returns to where he left his bag and munches the last of the sausages as he sits. The dog looks on, cocking her head.

"Eat."

Horst tosses a piece of the sausage to the dog.

Horst wearily stands, unfolds his jacket, spreading it on the ground under a huge tree just a few yards from the stream.

The dog approaches, circles, and finally lies next to him.

Horst shuts his eyes.

Silence.

Darkness.

Then movement. Eyes open. Horst's vision gains focus. He sees the trees above him. Eerily, the forest is dead silent. No crickets, cicadas, frogs nor sounds common to the night. He wonders what awakened him, as he is so exhausted.

The dog?

Slowly, he turns his head towards the stream on his right, just a few yards downslope, then left, at the embers of a fire.

A fire?

He doesn't recall making a fire.

Horst goes through in his mind the last few hours he was attempting to fish with a spear to no avail. He doesn't recall making a fire, but there it is, a few hours, it seems, warming him in the dead of night. He didn't make one, as he doesn't want to be seen.

He sits up, realizing this, and looks at the sleeping form of the shepherd.

Then he finally hears a sound. It is the sound of water. A movement making small splashes at the stream.

He wonders who has been there as he slept, as he crawls towards the source of the noise in the darkness.

Small pools of water make circles in the stream, disrupting its flow as it passes.

Like pebbles being dropped, but it is coming from beneath the water.

In the light of stars, Horst searches the ground for his self-made spear. He grabs it, standing now, hovering near the waterline.

Fish.

Small slivers of fish pass right under the transparent surface of the fresh water. Some, larger than others, are touching the surface, feeding, it seems.

Some are leaping over the surface.

With avid hunger, Horst plummets the spear at a fish. It skillfully evades him. Visions of the earlier adventure, which ended in frustration, flow through his mind.

But they weren't THIS close.

Hell-bent on eating, Horst repeatedly jabs at the fish as their silvery bodies evade him.

Again.

Again.

Again.

Sweat pours from his brow. He wipes it from his eyes.

The shepherd is awake now, watching, yelping and encouraging him.

Again.

Again.

Water splashes; the fish scatter.

Horst sits.

Exasperation fills his features.

He looks back at the embers.

He takes in a few breaths.

Horst mutters a prayer in German.

He shuts his eyes as if to meditate.

He opens his eyes and hears more splashes.

He goes deeper into the center of the stream where the splashes are more evident.

Fish jump.

What are they?

Horst aims and jabs at the water.

A fish is stunned, a fin caught.

It struggles as Horst follows it, jabbing, jabbing...

Right through the eye.

Horst grabs the slippery fish with both hands lest it slip.

Triumphantly he holds the fish.

The shepherd looks on from the shoreline, head cocked to one side.

"We got one!"

Horst returns to the shore, joyful in the simplicity of his triumph. He tosses the fish onto the embers.

Whoever made the fire made it right on time.

MORNING. The remains of the fish, charred eyes and head staring back, smoke in the gaining light of dawn. Horst is retying his dirty boots now caked in dirt. He looks up at the dog.

The shepherd dog walks briskly through the forest, following the stream. Horst attempts to follow despite the understory, which is constantly trapping his legs.

Finally, the dog pauses, sniffing, head down.

Horst opens a small steel compass. He sees the dog has been leading him south via the stream. Smart dog.

The dog looks up, as if attempting to communicate.

Suddenly, it takes off.

Horst follows, now intent on not losing the shepherd.

Reaching a clearing, Horst spots the dog lapping in the stream.

Horst descends, rolls up his pants, and stoops down to drink in the coolness. He looks up to locate the train trestle he saw the day before.

They're headed in the right direction.

He fills his water canteen once again, then washes his face.

Mud clings to his boots, now worn from his struggle to walk the endless miles of forest.

He sniffs his shirt caked with dirt, leaves and detritus. He must be quite a sight.

From far off, Horst can now hear the distinct sound of a train passing on the trestle.

The chug, chug of the engine fills him with ambivalence: Both hope and fear of detection mingle together. He observes the shepherd sitting, then rolling now on the quiet grass.

He relaxes, taking the animal's cue.

The dog keeps rolling, licking to clean her paws as she lies on her back, feeling safe around Horst.

Horst relaxes even further and proceeds to undress. He reciprocates the sense of safety.

With a meal in both their bellies, he decides it's time to wash, like every animal does afterwards.

The water is a warmth he didn't expect, flowing sedately across his tired skin and lulling him further.

Naked into the stream, he descends, washing off the dirt and with it, his history.

"I'm going to call you Manna."

The dog pauses, observing Horst, and in his own interpretation, she seems to smile.

Horst dips his head, opening his eyes to the underwater world of weeds, evading fish and a pebbly bottom. Slowly in gentle stride, he allows himself the luxury of the moment, making the moment last as if it were forever.

He surfaces and glances at Manna, who is now standing at attention, hairs on her back appearing to stand. It makes the shepherd even larger than she is.

Horst observes the ribs showing on Manna and makes a mental note to hunt game this time and to forage, to share his meal every time with this new companion who is his navigator. Not knowledgeable about plants, Horst realizes he needs to confine his diet to fish and small game, just in case he encounters a toxic plant. He wishes for Krista, knowledgeable with mushrooms and wild edible plants.

The dog darts a glance at Horst, darts a glance away in the direction of where the passing sound of the train originated. Quickly, Horst senses an urgency and dresses, tugging at his worn boots and shouldering his messenger bag.

Manna leads him into the woods, away from the stream. Someone Horst has not seen yet is coming.

Horst enters a profusion of trees, where the dog pauses, watching, pointing like a hunting dog. He takes the dog's cue and watches from his hidden position between the branches.

The sound of trucks, motors gaining.

A convoy of trucks and a tank. Men with hats in green

and brown. Horst squints. They're barely yards, even a few feet from Horst.

A red four-pointed star on a man's square hat. A woman sits perched on a truck, looking on with a few men. A lapel in green with two red stripes.

The red army.

Russians?

The convoy appears to be headed north whence he came from. Upstream, according to his map, as he opens it to determine their origin. Is the south already occupied?

Horst digs into his bag, revealing his identity papers as a German citizen, his picture showing a younger, wholesome man with a trim mustache, a well-tailored shirt. His working papers are in another sleeve, showing him as a tailor for the Nazis. It does not bode well for him if he were caught. Then he thinks of Agatha in happier times, her garden, their rented house, the village.

Then he thinks of Krista, his only child.

He pulls the plastic the working papers are in and toys with the idea of hiding it.

Emerging from the trees, he gestures to the shepherd and walks toward the road. He looks up and down, watching for movement.

Song birds flutter, gaining flight.

With thoughts of Krista on his mind, he quickly gains in step and heads down the road, Manna as his watchman.

43

KRISTA WATCHES the farmhouse door open, then the shed to her right. She has to lean down low behind the water pump, which gives little cover, if any. A young boy, about twelve, emerges from the shed. The hens cluck.

He looks up, almost making eye contact.

Krista quickly moves around the pump, attempting to hide. The boy, dusty from gathering hay, is carrying a bale and loading a horse cart. Busily, he clambers onto the back, rearranging, then steps off, re-entering the shed. Again, he emerges, filling the cart with crates of produce. Krista watches, curiously wondering whether it is market day. If he is going north with whoever is with him, she needs to get on that cart, giving her a much-needed rest... And perhaps new clothing that would allow her to toss her Nazi youth uniform.

A man, stocky, blond, bearded, emerges from a corner of the shed, pulling a horse with him. He connects the horse with the cart.

Good. That's MY ride, Krista muses. She ponders on how she wouldn't be seen, unless they are willing to help.

Krista has to be prepared for the questions. What are you doing here? Where did you come from? Are you running away from someone?

Her legs are growing tired from hunching in the same position. Soon, she knows the cramp will overcome her, and she has to stand.

A finger pokes her back.

Krista leaps.

A familiar face.

The girl is joyous.

"Mila?!"

The girl puts her fingers across her lips, signaling silence.

Then she embraces Krista.

A sense of belonging, of coming home, seizes Krista in a paroxysm of joy.

Mila inundates both cheeks with kisses, looks into her eyes as Krista's gales of laughter rouse the hens nearby.

Mila's infectious laughter in response rouses the boy from the shed.

He comes running in his dusty clothes, hay still clinging, his smile wide and hair full of life. All arms, legs and knees, too long for him.

He is about Krista's age.

The two girls leap up and down, arms linked, and the boy, without awaiting an explanation, joins in.

Hens fly, cluck, and sheep join in the medley of unbridled laughter.

From the farmhouse in the distance, a door swings open, and the stocky man emerges.

He darts towards the group with a limp.

Mila waves at the stocky man, broad-shouldered and handsome in his early forties as his features become more distinct with his approach.

"Edgar, this is my sister, Krista."

Edgar studies Krista in her filthy Nazi youth uniform. His smile fades.

The boy looks from father to Krista and back, searching for an explanation in the heavy pause.

"I – I'm – WAS a Nazi youth teacher. I –"

Mila interrupts, her slur as a disabled child giving away her anxiety. "She had to do it to survive."

Krista nods vehemently in agreement. The boy smiles and raises a hand in greeting.

"I am Holzer."

"Hello, Holzer. I defected. Ran away to find my father, who has been taken..."

Edgar places his hand on Krista's shoulder. "Come. Breakfast is waiting."

44

WHAT KRISTA UNDERSTANDS as the story unfolds about Mila's escape is a man awakened Mila from the edge of a river. Mila, in her halting way, still exuberant from their reunion, tells Krista over a large breakfast of her narrow and fearful escape with the aid of Edgar and his son, Holzer.

As Hannah, a Jewish woman in her fifties, makes a hearty breakfast of fresh eggs from the henhouse and a ham still hanging from the rafters, Mila's account takes over the atmosphere of the large stone kitchen. Edgar and Holzer add to the story, helping Mila with her memory.

Mila, having fainted, was shaken awake from the abattoir around her by a wounded man: Edgar. Mila's confusion added to her turmoil as she sat riveted to the sounds of the dying and the detritus of the dead strewn all around in the aftermath of a massacre. Edgar, a prisoner of war, had managed to escape from a concentration camp and came upon the river to drink, only to witness the firing squad that annihilated an entire population of civilians with some form of disability.

Holzer is a German boy, disabled with some form of genetic disorder that makes his arms and legs too large for him. He was among the lineup with Krista, as he did not "fit" with the perfection the Nazis expected. Among them, but managing to hide before the lineup was made, was Hannah, the Jewish woman who is now making breakfast for her makeshift family. Her own family is among the dead.

Whereas the exuberance of reunion lifts them to a sense of buoyancy, the account makes the mood heavier in the room. Edgar explains that after walking for miles away from the death scene by night, they finally came to a deserted farm where the animals, to their joy, were still alive. Edgar had been a farmer in England and knew how to sustain a farm with the help of his new "son", Holzer. When they saw their fortune, they dared not question the fate of the former owners and thanked the divine grace of God for their luck.

Krista feels she completes this new family, their graciousness and warmth making her feel welcome and touched. She feels herself relaxing after endless weeks of trudging in fear and hunger through the forest. She tells them of her encounters with the girl she believes is the ghost of the former tenant's daughter. In the splendid mansion that was given to them when her father was appointed tailor to the regime, her parents had come to sense that the Nazis had been murdering and plundering the previous families to give away the houses and their contents to their cronies.

No one comments as a hush falls on the room.

They eat in companionable silence for the rest of the meal.

45

Horst follows the road strewn with rocks and pockmarked by heavy artillery. A sense of dread lingers in the air. The shepherd leads the way, a few yards ahead. He glances at his compass. Still heading south.

Ahead, the road wends its way into the forest, quiet, grim, foreboding. Night is descending again as Horst notes the time on his water-fogged watch. He pauses to wind it, but it is obviously broken with the water from the streams and the river he was drenched in. He notes the upscale German insignia of the brand, a Nazi eagle embossed under the thick watch face. Despite the make, water still breached the watch.

Thoughts of better times with parties at the shop, where the German military officers were invited to see fashionable clothing for men and women, flow through his mind. He thinks about the time he received the watch as a gift from Kommandant Beyer, what they were dining on, the opulent dining rooms he ended up frequenting, and the celebrations with Agatha on their anniversary and birthdays.

Agatha.

Grief assails him like a sharp bullet, tearing through his now thin frame, causing him to stumble. His eyes begin to brim with tears, and in a split-second decision, he turns towards the forest, sensing a desire to hide, perhaps to roll into a ball and sleep away the despair that is overtaking him.

Manna senses the change of his pace, turns and follows Horst into the woods. The dog whines about her disagreement, and Horst pauses, leaning down to pet the dog as she approaches.

The chug, chug of an approaching train in the distance once again signals how much progress Horst has made.

They are closer to the tracks now. He considers the plan for getting a ride, but looks down at the shepherd he can't leave behind.

He follows Manna, who leads again, deeper into the wood, but still going south. At all costs, he decides he will take her with him. Perhaps he will find a train with an empty animal stall, which would be safer. Just to help him ease his blistered feet.

Horst looks up at the approaching twilight, opens his bag, and decides to make camp. As he assembles wood and kindling for the fire, the shepherd watches. He sits nurturing the embers and thinks idly of who made a fire for him not too long ago. The fish is long gone, so Horst stands to assess where he can find food.

As Horst pulls his flask from the bag, he sips it sparingly and offers some to Manna. The dog turns her head as if to refuse, then stands and darts away. Horst quickly follows, wondering.

As Horst follows, he smells rain, and upon inspection, Horst comes upon a pond. He washes his face, noting the algae.

"Can't drink this one, Manna."

The dog cocks her head to the side and sits as if to ponder.

Then movement. Horst instinctively pulls out his homemade spear and ducks as he turns. A rabbit, its nose moving, sensing danger.

Manna gives chase, and as she does, a piece of silver, round like a coin, pings from her collar. Horst walks over and picks it up, noting it is a dog tag: Phoebe.

He looks up, quickly following the shepherd. "Phoebe! Your name is Phoebe!"

The shepherd sharply turns at the sound of her name, then resumes running as Horst gives chase. Phoebe is gaining on the rabbit; then it plummets into a hole. Phoebe pauses over the hole, barking, whining, tail wagging. Horst walks over, pocketing the tag, consoling the dog.

"It's okay, Phoebe. We'll find another."

But Phoebe again snaps to attention and is looking into the distance, almost pointing.

Horst follows the dog's eyes and looks.

Another stream flows near the bottom of a cliff.

Horst surveys the area where a stiff wind blows,

heralding rain as clouds gather in a dark brew. Quickly, he follows the dog into the clearing, his spear drawn and ready to fish again.

46

KRISTA DIPS her head under the tub's warmth, a bar of soap in one hand. Mila's tender hands, plump and soft, rub a cloth on her back, soapy and sudsy. Nearby, a simple dress hangs on a hanger, waiting for Krista.

Mila is humming a song, the same one Krista was singing the day they were gardening and Mila disappeared, sensing she was endangering her benefactors. Krista hums along and finally sings the tune, which makes Mila smile and giggle.

Krista feels comforted by the warmth of the house, its tenants, and the joy of finding Mila. She hopes it is a matter of time before she finds their parents as well. In the reverie, Krista finds herself nodding off, watching as if in a dream the face of Mila as she hums and washes her hair.

Soon, they are done, and Krista emerges from the bath, Mila helping her wrap herself in a thick towel. A timid knock, then Holzer's round face appears, averting his eyes in shyness.

"Dinner's ready."

Mila squeals with delight and almost forgets Krista, who stands wrapped in a towel, barefooted.

"Oops!" Mila laughs. She grabs a pair of pink slippers and plops them by Krista's side as she impishly joins the boy at the threshold.

"See you at dinner!"

Krista nods, slipping her swollen and blistered feet into the soft slippers. She wonders how she will walk down the stairs, but she remembers fondly how Mila becomes forgetful when food presents itself. She chuckles. As she exits the bathroom, she is grateful Holzer stands by waiting to assist her down the steps.

A roasted chicken, small potatoes in butter, and a medley of carrots and asparagus sit on the trestle table. Edgar pours milk from the cows, the cream still on top, in several glasses.

He hands one to Mila, then Krista as she sits.

Hannah brings out a small cake with buttercream frosting and places it nearby on a sideboard. It makes Krista drool, as she has not seen such lavishness since she left Frau Dieterstrasse's home months before. *This one*, she thinks, *is better, as it is all made with loving hands instead of a local bakery, the milk from the cows just yards away in the barn.*

She is seated next to Mila, facing the open window with a view of the cliff she was perched on just a few days ago. Just like old times in their village house. The pastoral scene of the hens safely in their shed for the night, the sheep standing idly, and the cows in the barn makes the room feel so secure. They pass the dishes around, all content with the world.

The self-created family passes the evening reading stories from books out loud. No Nazi books about Hitler, but classics from far-off Denmark and Italian books with fancy pictures. Mila reads the German fairy tales in her singsong voice as Krista marvels how well she can read. Hannah plays the violin later on as Mila makes tea. The music and the tea lull Krista, and before she knows it, her head is nodding, beckoned by much-needed sleep.

Mila nudges Krista to wakefulness as the embers from the fireplace begin to take hold, and Holzer stands to turn on the lamps for Hannah to better see her notes from the music stand.

Edgar claps his hands, his British accent resonating as he asks for an encore. Laughter.

Mila gives Hannah a peck on the cheek as Krista thanks her hosts for the hospitality.

Mila ascends the stairs with Krista, whose hike through the forests has taken a toll on her young feet. Krista makes it to the top step, almost faltering into Mila's supportive embrace. The girl escorts her to a small, but comfortable room with a simple dresser, a nightstand, and a bed with a handmade coverlet.

The sounds of cicadas chorus through the open window framing the view beyond of the forests that Krista made her approach from. Mila slides off the soft down-quilted slippers she gave Krista, exposing her now bleeding feet. The warm bath temporarily assuaged the pain, but several weeks of walking in the boots, which were meant for special occasions not rough terrain, show on the teenager's feet. Mila stands and returns to the bathroom. She notes Mila has not changed, although she appears happier and more buoyant. Almost too carefree.

Krista worries that their peace and joy will be short-lived, but the little family seems very calm on their little farm. Krista makes a note to ask the next day why Edgar and Holzer were loading the horse cart when she was greeted unexpectedly by Mila. It appeared that they were readying for a trip and taking provisions.

Mila returns with a warm bowl of sudsy water and a clean towel. Kneeling before Krista, she washes her feet, then opens a creamy ointment, which she applies to Krista's injured feet. Krista marvels at Mila's skill, noting how the girl expertly wraps both her feet in bandages and secures them so that they are snug.

"And how am I supposed to get around now that they're all wrapped up, missy?" Krista's tone is playful.

Mila looks back at Krista from where she kneels. "You're not going anywhere. Not without our help."

"Aren't we going to look for my parents? Your parents?"

Behind the bed, a breeze blows the curtains in from the open window.

Mila eyes her with doleful eyes. "Not until your feet are well."

A pause.

Then Mila turns away, folding Krista's newly mended uniform, and begins humming a song that sounds so familiar to Krista that it lulls her into a deep sleep.

47

THE FIRE IS LARGER than Horst wanted, but there is a distinct chill in the nighttime air after the rain. Phoebe sits nearby, watching. Fish bones and heads litter the area around the fire. The two shared several fish, now expertly speared by Horst and charred in the fire.

Earlier, in the darkness beyond the small opening in the forest, Horst saw a small path, which appeared to lead towards a tunnel and the train tracks above, set on a hill. In the dimming light, Horst thought the tunnel was still too far for Horst to assess if it was some type of underground bunker or storage for armaments. He doesn't want to be caught there, surprising a troop of soldiers from either the Reich or the Red army. He wonders if the path has been used recently and makes a mental note to examine it before he emerges onto it. It should tell him if the tunnel is in use.

Horst darted well away from the path and camped past

a copse of trees and undergrowth so he was hidden not just from the elements, but from anyone who may pass the path. There, he cooked the fish in the open fire and shared it with the dog. Now done and sated, by the light of the crackling fire, he calls to Phoebe, who comes over, head down in submission.

He pets the shepherd, who appears healthier now, her coat glinting in the moonlight. He digs in his pocket for her tag, which she dropped earlier when she ran, and reattaches it on the collar. The collar is made of leather, matted with dirt and hair. On the spur of the moment, he decides to remove it from the shepherd's neck. Phoebe willingly lets her new master remove it, trusting him and licking his face as he stands to wash it at the stream.

The metal gleams as Horst washes the collar, now noting the collar is also matted with blood. He washes it away, wipes the collar with his shirt, and lets it dry on a rock by the stream.

Phoebe watches Horst return to her side and inspect her fur by the firelight, noting any scratches or any past injuries. He brings out some tincture of iodine in anticipation of any open sores or injuries. Horst sees a gash on her side as he parts her fur to comb it with his hands. It appears healed, and the fur has obliterated any sign of injury.

Phoebe licks her master's hands in gratitude as Horst continues to comb her fur with his fingers.

Then Phoebe's ears perk up, hearing what Horst has to wait to hear.

Phoebe stands.

Another train is coming.

This one is not as fast, and the chug, chug, chug of the wheels gives away its laboring movements as it wends its way on the tracks.

Is it slowing?

Horst glances at the fire and swiftly covers it with dirt to obscure his position lest the train stop. He has to determine if there are dining cars, usually well-lit from within, which would show him Germans in uniform dining at leisure or Russians celebrating the takeover. He has no one to get news from as far as the status of the war.

Horst grabs his messenger bag and darts towards the sound of a train whistle. The path, strewn with rocks and tree limbs, has obviously not been used for some time. That is good. Under cover of darkness, they walk carefully on the path, Phoebe leading the way.

The path wends its way deep into the forest. Horst walks by the moonlight and the stars, but several minutes into the walk, the trees become dense, the branches obscuring any light provided by the sky.

Horst pauses and Phoebe turns to await his decision. A sense of desolation and unexplained malice assails him. It tastes like copper in his mouth and exudes a scent of sulfur. Horst feels very alone and becomes sensitive to a keening sound, as if someone or some animal is crying. A very low tone, but unmistakable.

He surveys the impenetrable darkness, the path now hidden ahead. Behind him, in the distance where he originated, there is a low light from where the trees allow the sky to light the way. Somehow, where he stands now appears more remote, which doesn't make sense to Horst, as the tracks are closer now and thus closer to civilization. Hopefully, one that would be welcome to him, though he remains unsure.

But he is alone with his thoughts, a creeping, gnawing fear, and a shepherd who is awaiting him faithfully. The keening continues. Seized by an internal alarm, Horst turns back, walking now with resolve to return to his campsite, where he snuffed the fire.

Horst ignores another train whistle, this time the chugging going faster to indicate that it is obviously running full speed towards a destination going south.

As the sound of the chugging recedes in the depths of the forest, Horst finds a light in the trees, which, upon inspection, are the embers from his fire.

The fear, malice and despair within his psyche lessen with every step. He wonders whether his subconscious or something outside of him is somehow warning him that the path was not to be taken. Still quaking somewhat from the inexplicable fear, he battles with indecision as to whether he can risk making another fire. The darkness makes him want light.

He makes a new fire. The light and warmth lessen the sense of menace and isolation. Horst listens for any sounds. He can no longer hear keening. As he rolls his messenger bag under his head near the fire, he calls it a night and resolves to discover by daylight, with a clear head and the clarity of the sun, why the path filled him with terror. Yes, it was terror, upon introspection. A wave of fear that almost left him paralyzed.

Phoebe walks around in circles and then presses her back to him, further warming Horst and exuding an aura of comfort and safety.

He sleeps.

48

Krista is stunned. Mila explains she is sure her parents are both dead, murdered. She and Edgar of course will escort her, Mila says, in a matter-of-fact way, to the train platform with Krista dressed in her green dress. The Russians are not kind to Nazi Youth, so they burned her uniform. The Russians leave the ordinary citizens alone, particularly the disabled; and of course, are receptive to their allies like the British. Edgar tells Krista she can ride the train all the way north to the army installation at Budingen where the Frau told her her father is stationed under duress. But Mila would not, or could not, go with her.

Why?

Krista thinks she misunderstands, but Mila explains and explains again that she has to stay or possibly be caught by any remaining German soldiers who are still killing any Jews or "non-Aryans" when they can. She fears the disability so clear in her eyes will risk her life once again.

Finally, Krista understands and feels guilty for being insensitive to Mila's plight.

After the warmth and relative safety of the farm, the company of people who are also outcasts, as she sees herself to be, Krista finds herself alone in her quest again. As she sits in the wooden horse cart that she saw being loaded by Holzer a few days ago, she feels trepidation of what lies ahead. She watches the horse's head bob to and fro as it clops down the dusty lane, Edgar sitting right behind it at the reins and Mila facing her in the wagon amongst the produce.

Krista is torn. If she stays, she will never reach her father or find out if her mother is still alive. If she goes, she will lose Mila. She wants them all together, but now she must brave it again. Alone.

Why must life be this way?

During the ride, Krista selfishly begs Mila to reconsider. She knows now what she needs to do in order for them to thrive in the woods. Mila has good boots on and so does she, a pair that fits her perfectly. Again, just like the handsome house given to them by the Reich, the clothes and shoes were from the previous tenants of the farm, who seemed to have abandoned the animals in their haste to run. Krista recounts her odyssey to Mila, how she ate berries, all types of leaves, particularly clover, which is bitter to the taste, but very edible. Mila keeps shaking her head no. Then, for the rest of the ride to the station, Mila hums a tune that Agatha used to sing as she embroidered.

"Don't you miss Agatha, Mila?"

Mila gives Krista a look that gives away the depth of her loss, the deep anguish that comes almost like a blow to her gut, over and over again until she can no longer stand.

The cart rolls on inexorably to their fate.

49

THE SUN STANDS BRIGHT, almost at a zenith by the time Horst refastens Phoebe's collar and gives the dog a quick rubdown. Packed and boots cushioned with leaves to ease his feet, he once again enters the path, carrying his spear.

The forest darkens as Horst delves down the winding path. Yards later, Horst looks back from where he came and again notes the discernible difference in light, the bright sun now but a halo in the distance between trees.

Today it is quieter as Horst listens for the sounds of trains passing. He wonders if it is a Sunday, when only a few trains would pass at this hour. He arrives shortly at where he stopped the night before to turn back, fear alarming his senses, the sound of keening heralding doom.

This time, undeterred by fatigue and braved by a bright sun past the shade, Horst moves forth, watching his step. He wonders if the sense of fear might be an internal caution to watch for mines. He looks down, examining the ground as he goes. Phoebe sniffs the ground as if mimicking her master, looking up to check on Horst and then moving forward again.

Deeper into the path, vegetation takes over as the ground makes way for dead leaves and trees that appeared to creep. Large roots cover the ground and make passing difficult. Horst senses in the darkness, which is again gaining as he moves forward, something ominous. This time he is determined to reach the tunnel and investigate. He hopes that up close he can see better if the passing trains carry passengers without soldiers or one that carries supplies where he and Phoebe can ride under cover.

Suddenly, Horst hears the unmistakable sound of a train blasting its way just a few yards from his position. Surprised at its closeness, he pauses to take in what is ahead. The vines of trees cover the walls of the tunnel that supports the tracks. As he gingerly approaches, he sees he is a few yards from what appears to be the right arch of the tunnel's mouth.

The shepherd stops, seeming to listen to the approaching train and gazing at Horst. Horst surveys the high arch as he slowly moves towards the mouth of the deep tunnel. A light showing the way out on the other end gives him more confidence.

As the train approaches from above him, Horst backs away to gain a view of the passing train. It slows as Horst signals the dog with a finger to remain silent.

Cattle cars pass one right after another, the wheels screeching as it chugs. One black car after another with a small barred window.

Then the train slows.

Suddenly, a car slides open, and a young girl in her teens, blonde, swiftly jumps out, followed by another with flowing dark hair.

A keening.

A thud.

Horst stands rooted to the spot, just a few feet from where the blonde girl landed.

Then the other girl, a woman – hanging from a tree, her neck broken, her eyes glazing as she chokes.

Then she stiffens and is still.

Horst hears Phoebe going crazy, barking.

Horst quickly approaches the blonde girl lying on the ground, but blood quickly pools from her head, her eyes shut.

Horst leaps back in horror.

It is Mila.

The train above him gains momentum; the cattle car slams shut.

It moves, screeching, heading north.

Mila lies motionless, body broken in a blue dress rapidly soaking in red.

The keening comes again, but it comes from none other than Horst's lips, a cry of loss and horror.

50

KRISTA EMERGES from the back of the cart, Mila right at her heels. She has finally convinced Mila to go, and Edgar looks on quietly, unable to protest. Mila is, after all, like a sister to Krista. Mila extends both her hands to hug Edgar, who hugs her back, his back stiff. He is without emotion, like a soldier doing his duty, which he is.

The station is busy, but in the corner of her eye, Krista spots a group of German soldiers hurriedly shuffling some women into a train car without windows. The women look exhausted, emaciated even, and are all wearing the same ill-fitting pajamas, or so it appears. Striped gray and white pajamas, like prisoners. Krista puzzles over this, as she knows the Russians are gaining on Germany. To what extent, she does not know.

Edgar quickly ushers her into a passenger car, her identification as a Nazi Youth mentor clutched in her left hand just in case, her pack on her right.

Krista climbs the steps onto the train and turns to

reach down for Mila. Suddenly, a whistle, heralding the train's imminent departure, makes Edgar turn away.

Then he is gone.

Krista looks right and left, searching.

Mila has also disappeared.

The train yanks, pushes, and then it is slowly but perceptibly moving.

Krista steps down, trying to locate Mila.

"Mila! Mila!"

The train gains momentum, and she feels an arm reach down for her, pulling her like a rag doll back onto the train.

"Here!" (In German.)

A German soldier has her in his arms, his kind face smiling with congeniality as he protects her from the open door.

Krista, taken aback, wordlessly steps in, still looking back out the door for Mila.

"There's no one out there, Fraulein."

The soldier tips his hat, walks down the train corridor and Krista follows, her identity papers in one hand. She reaches for the soldier, a man in his early twenties, who appears very kind. "A girl of fourteen was with me. Blonde hair, blue..."

The soldier stops and turns, taken aback. "Except for an elderly man and his wife, who took the other train, there was no one on the platform but you, Fraulein."

"Surely she's now here in the car..."

Krista dashes past the soldier, surveying and darting

from one cabin to the next, opening it, then the next, to the consternation of passengers inside.

A conductor in uniform, a swastika on his lapel, blocks her way as the soldier behind her gives chase.

"Please stop, Fraulein!" The conductor has both hands raised to block her.

"She was with me on the platform!"

The conductor eyes the soldier behind Krista. "Your ticket, please?!"

Krista shows him her papers as a Nazi Youth teacher.

The conductor's face softens. He hands it back to her.

The soldier steps in. "She was alone and was getting a ticket... but..."

The conductor dismissively waves a hand. "Not a problem. You can share a cabin at the end. I didn't see those papers. There may be Russians embarking at the next stop."

With that, the soldier ushers Krista into an empty cabin, shuts the door, and removes his uniform, revealing a civilian shirt.

The train platform sits empty, the train receding into the distance. The sound of its motor fades as it moves away.

Behind the station, an abandoned horse cart sits without a horse, bales of hay long gone, the fruit boxes empty.

Where Edgar sat, dried blood stains the seat and the ground below. On one side, more dried blood on the ground where it pooled. It appears it dried in the sun several months ago.

51

MILA COULDN'T BREATHE INSIDE the cattle car. Summer's undulating heat stifled her as she clambered past the emaciated women, dirty in their pyjamas. A soldier had forced her with a rifle, laughing, into the car. She had been courageous enough to go with Edgar and Holzer to the market, stopping at the train station to sell the rest of the fruit to passengers. Now she was squeezed in with women who appeared in shock, too weak to cry.

She clambered over the bodies of women in pajamas, reaching for the door, which was secured with a latch. The train gained momentum. A woman in rags with long dark hair sat by the door. She reached for the latch. She was stronger than Mila despite her emaciated condition, wearing what appeared to be a dog collar. The latch gave, and the sliding door made of wood slowly slid open.

Who would have known that anyone would have spotted her eyes and Holzer's irregular frame as they stood with the remaining crates of peaches? Edgar had stood nearby and watched for soldiers, when suddenly they appeared with a mass of concentration camp survivors, attempting to load an entire contingent into a filthy cattle car.

Edgar had signaled to the two teens to pick up the crate to depart when the worst had happened. He had miscalculated. Certainly, he thought, the Russians were freeing the camps of survivors. Maybe they have not reached their village.

He turned and bolted for the cart, reaching it when a few shots rang out. He reached up to grab the reins from the horse and sat, but everything went black.

He heard fireworks and wondered as he faded what the party was about.

Holzer was near the wagon, his blood jettisoning all over the sides of the cart. German soldiers descended on the fruit, taking the remains of the produce and unharnessing the horse.

They got the horse free, and one led it to join another soldier nearby, who beamed at their new ride.

The soldier continued beaming and inspected the cart as his comrades left, eager to eat the fruit. As people eagerly ascended to take the remaining vegetables from the back of the cart, the young soldier surveyed the area.

Slowly, he reached for the deserted bridle, placing it over his head. With one deft movement, he pulled his uniform shirt off, exposing a white undershirt.

He pulled the cart away as the people left.

52

HORST AWAKENS, and it is twilight. He must have fainted, he surmises. Horst looks at the body above him, the long telltale hair. She was a brunette. Rags of clothing in stripes of gray and what looked to be white a long while ago hang tattered and molding. A collar of what appears as leather, like the dog's, is strapped to her neck. That odd article of clothing seems to have caught on a branch, strangling her as she volleyed down from the train.

A failed escape.

If she had fallen to the ground, she would have been killed anyway, right next to Mila.

Was it Mila?

Is he dreaming?

It was just a few hours ago.

Horst gingerly approaches the body, already in a state of advanced decomposition.

Yes, it is real.

Blonde hair with long bangs obscure the eyes.

The body is mostly skeletal.

Horst moves away, vomiting, as flies fly around the body.

Phoebe, head down, walks towards the body and pulls something from it. A small notebook, soiled and torn.

Horst looks up, breathing with one hand over his nose as he watches the dog approach him.

Phoebe puts it down, wagging her tail.

A photo, wet and muddy, falls out.

A young boy stands in front of a cart.

Horst picks it up, examines it.

He drops it.

He puts his hands on the sides of his head as if to screen out what he is seeing.

And cries.

He gathers leaves, twigs, anything he can find. He covers Mila's body with them like a parent tucking a child in for the night. He sobs through it all, looking up once in a while to note where the woman's body is hanging above him.

He doesn't want her to fall on him.

He shivers and sobs as he works, until finally, Mila is part of the trees and the forest, forever in slumber.

Then, with the deepness of the tunnel still ahead, he points the dog in the direction of his old camp, where once again he seeks the refuge of familiarity. A fire, some fish and a place to sleep next to Phoebe.

A handkerchief lies on the ground, the embroidered

flower lending a hint of the sweetness of the life that is now extinguished. Then a breeze blows, blowing the leaves and the handkerchief – to rest atop Mila's covered body.

53

Krista awakens to the shrill sound of the train's brakes screeching. She sits up and surveys the small cabin, where the young German soldier has changed into a shirt and tie, no uniform. He is casually looking out the window like any other passenger as the train slows at a platform.

She looks inquiringly at him.

He smiles. "Oberweid."

"I'm halfway there!"

"To where?"

Krista doesn't want to divulge her ultimate destination to a stranger. Instead, she stands and prepares to leave.

"Thank you for your kindness. I must go."

Krista exits the cabin and almost runs into two young Russian soldiers. She slips past without comment, but one grabs her arm. "Anyone in there with you?"

Thinking quickly, Krista replies, "My boyfriend, but I'm leaving him."

The two soldiers glance at each other and chuckle. One taps his head with a grin. They walk on.

Krista turns away, darting past other passengers with a grin.

It worked.

Out on the platform, a few armed Russian soldiers are watching a group of passengers exit the train. Krista moves quickly, pretending she is late. She quickly surveys the area – blonde girls, tall handsome men, vendors... and vegetable sellers.

No sight of Mila or Edgar. No Holzer.

Krista's face crumples, almost in tears. Perhaps Mila never meant to be on the train with her, and she has to accept that.

Krista crosses the street behind the station and notes the village signs. North.

She steps onto a narrow lane and begins walking in earnest. Then she realizes she is lost.

Krista glances at the train station, crosses again and returns to the side of the station. The tracks wind their way into the forest. A signpost shows several directions. One points to Eisenach.

She turns and follows, going parallel to the tracks.

She digs into her pockets, searching.

She looks down at the photograph of Mila and her at the birthday party.

She trudges on.

The tracks wend through the deep forest, the undergrowth preventing Krista from walking too fast. She struggles over some vines, almost falling. She was replenished and restocked by Mila's new "family" and feels a modicum of comfort knowing her pack holds nuts, cheese, sausages and a cake. Fresh rolls filled the basket given to her by the Frau, tucked in with a waxen cheesecloth to protect it from the elements. The water in a bottle now makes the pack heavier.

Nightfall is heralded by cawing crows, signaling a field where she can perhaps rest. Sure enough, as she turns the bend following the tracks, a train chugs in the distance adjacent to an open field where rows of corn grow in abundance. The train goes faster as the engine gains uphill and is soon receding in the distance. Krista looks behind her as another train, this one headed in the direction she wants, due north, marches its way towards her.

Krista considers a ride again, but the station is at least half a mile away. Her blistered feet are not completely healed. As the northbound train passes her, it appears to be slowing down. But it only holds cattle cars. She moves away and watches it as it ambles past, lights now on in the growing dusk.

Then the train slows perceptibly, parallel to the rows of corn. Krista walks faster, hoping she can hazard another ride, perhaps not in the comfort of a passenger cabin, but at least the cattle car would allow her feet and legs some rest and more ground covered in less time. She regrets stepping off the other one for fear of being questioned, but it was moot.

She approaches a cattle car, then another, searching for one that may be open or ajar. She will need to reach for the handle and climb two steps to enter. It slows.

Then the hairs on Krista's head begin to tingle. Deep in her stomach, something is dreadfully wrong. Dead silence. No crows caw, no wind, no sounds of the field and no murmurs of people. She pauses, now just a few feet from a car whose door appears ajar. From one of the barred windows, a keening sound.

She smells it before she sees it, carried by a breeze that blows from the train. Sick to her stomach, she backs away. Her eyes glued to the cars, she smells decay, putrefaction and human loneliness like a discarded rag.

Then she hears the crying, the wailing and the sound of fear from within.

She runs.

In the distance, she spots a valley, then – a tunnel.

She bolts for it, dropping her basket of rolls in her haste to make as much distance as she can from what she gleaned is an abattoir within the train cars.

The basket lies on the ground.

The cheese cloth parted as it fell, revealing the rolls. The fabric itself is molded and dusty.

Flies fly around the rolls, covering them. Where there are spots open, mold grows and maggots crawl.

Krista dashes back to retrieve it and sees.

It has only been a day or two since she received it from the kindly British farmer, Edgar.

Krista recoils in horror.

She drops the basket and continues running, confused, terrified, bewildered.

54

HORST ENTERS the tunnel with his lantern, shivers, and takes in his surroundings. Water drips from the dark ceiling, mildew on the walls and pools stagnant on the ground. He swings the lamp around to check the sides of the tunnel. A pair of eyes look back at him ahead. Horst gasps.

It is Phoebe.

Horst signals the dog to keep going.

He gingerly walks by the lantern light, willing himself to keep going lest he be tempted to turn back again and confront the bodies of Mila and the woman hanging from a tree.

This time, he is going to go through no matter how dark it becomes and see what is on the other end.

The dog pauses to await Horst, ever so faithful. Horst mutters soothingly in German, a practice he's been following to calm both himself and the dog.

It is more for himself, actually.

Halfway in, Horst realizes that the tunnel is deeper than he thought. He pauses once again to illuminate his surroundings, watching for any doors that might lead to an inner room where a soldier or two might be stationed.

All that meets him are frogs and a vole or two, scampering away from the unwelcome light of his lantern. The chorus of frogs reaches a crescendo as he gets closer to the midpoint and then begins to fade behind him.

Then, ahead, where the tunnel ends, a light.

Riveted to the light, Horst shuts off his lantern, plummeting him in darkness.

Phoebe howls, then lets out a bark.

The light at the end moves, then goes dark.

Phoebe dashes forward, barking.

Horst blindly follows.

He trips.

He lands on his chin, sending stars to his eyes.

"Phoebe!"

The dog pauses, wagging its tail.

The light comes on.

A man leans down, petting the dog.

He looks up.

Horst stands, recognizing a familiar face.

It is none other than the village bread man's son.

"Josef?!"

"Herr Schneider?!"

Horst approaches, rubbing a knee, as Josef darts over, turning his lantern on.

Dirt, dried blood, mud.

His shirt is partly torn; his beard appears unkempt, oily.

Josef's blond hair is a study in whorls and punctuated by twigs.

Horst studies Josef with amazement by the lantern light.

The men reach each other and hug.

Josef has aged. "I escaped."

Horst mentally puts two and two together as he stares down at the man's German-issued boots, the open shirt collar of a sergeant.

"The Russians. You must get rid of the uniform."

Josef nods solemnly.

Josef wearily removes the shirt, exposing a white undershirt. The man appears spent and older. Horst escorts him towards the edge of the tunnel, opening his flask of water.

They sit.

"I still have the bread cart. Outside."

Horst nods. He looks relieved.

Horst opens a package of fish he dried and offers it. He starts laughing with relief.

"You STILL have the bread cart?!" This Horst says in disbelief.

Josef wolfs down the dried fish. "Yes." He nods vigorously.

"Oops!" Horst replies. "And I have fish!"

They laugh together.

Horst pauses. He touches Josef's arm, hands, and his filthy hair.

Josef stops laughing. He keeps chewing, watching with a questioning look.

"I want to make sure you're truly alive."

Josef starts laughing again. He is seized with laughter.

"Are you?!" Josef ventures in return.

Horst offers an arm for Josef to touch.

"I am!"

Gales of laughter.

It's been a long time since Horst laughed.

Then Horst realizes he just saw Josef's photo as a child among Mila's belongings.

At the other end of the tunnel.

55

KRISTA TRUDGES with exhaustion towards the tunnel and thinks she hears men laughing. Bats swoop over her head and enter the tunnel ahead. She feels trepidation at what awaits her. She pauses, listening.

Laughter.

Then, as the bats enter, silence.

A swatting sound.

"Behind you."

The voice is in German.

Carefully now, she ventures forth from the brush, still carrying her canvas pack. She is seized by curiosity, but then backs away in fear.

Krista's thoughts swirl about her. *What if they're ghosts?* The surreal past few days left her in disquiet, a sense of foreboding and anxiety.

How much more must she interact with the dead? She listens to what sounds like men swatting at the bats, who laugh as if the war is over. Or are their senses gone? Have they gone mad? Have they abandoned all hope for the safety of insanity? Was she a witness to Mila's last few days on the farm? Or did Mila truly change her mind and leave her at the station?

Krista thinks of the basket and its moldy contents. She sits, now unsure of how prepared she is to investigate the tunnel like she did with the farm. She wonders if she should take a detour past the tunnel... more miles she doesn't need.

She deliberates her options.

Krista turns towards a row of trees, deciding to hide until the safety of morning.

Then another male voice issues from the tunnel. Snatches of conversation in German. The sound grabs her attention.

This one sounded VERY familiar.

More ghosts from the past.

"Why must you torment me?"

Krista weeps. Anger takes over her psyche, thoughts of revenge against the Nazis for casting away her family, destroying and leaving her to wander alone.

Alone.

To wander.

Then a bark.

Something is coming through the brush towards her.

A fox breaks through the brush.

Krista stands.

A German shepherd follows, giving chase.

"Phoebe!"

Instantly, Krista's eyes widen. She recognizes the voice immediately.

Her father.

A man emerges from the tunnel, looking out.

Krista sees him.

Speechless, she emerges from the brush.

The man sees Krista.

He is older, bedraggled, scruffy, exhausted.

He reaches out his arms in shock, then joy.

"Papa?!"

He dashes towards her, and she meets him.

He looks her in the eyes, both hands on her shoulders.

"Is this real?!"

Horst touches Krista's face, her dress, her arms.

"Papa... are you alive?!"

Horst nods vigorously, giving in to tears.

Krista's knees give out.

"Please. Let this be real!"

She cries as he kneels and holds her. Josef emerges from the tunnel with a joyous smile on his face.

Phoebe returns with a rabbit in her jaws, joining the group.

"Yes, daughter. I am alive! WE are alive!"

Laughter and tears.

Josef joins them, and they huddle with the dog.

They are barely five miles from the border of Austria.

56

JOSEF MAKES a fire within the shelter of trees in a small clearing a few yards from the train tunnel.

It has been an eventful evening. The rabbit, which Horst skinned, is roasting on the fire; a pot of hot water for tea sits simmering. Three army mugs wait in a line.

Horst is making another spear, this time for both Krista and Josef. Krista emerges from the woods with armfuls of clover, their vegetable for the meal. Krista eyes Josef's bread cart.

Krista plops the clover leaves near the simmering metal pot and approaches the cart. She runs her hands on the cart's edges, walking around it until she sees the leather-covered seat. There is no horse attached.

"It's truly not my old bread cart. I happened upon it."

Krista turns to Josef. The last time she saw him was when he was in his early teens. Lines on his face and under his eyes show he looks older than his seventeen years.

"Where was it?"

"At a train station in '43 – has it been a year? More? Someone in our platoon shot the driver and his son. Someone stole the horse."

Krista gaped. "WHICH train station?!"

"I – I – We were on patrol for some Jews who escaped. I think they were pretending to be German farmers, the former owners. I was told to take the cart. It held fruits and some veg..."

"WHICH station?!"

Horst approaches, placing his hands on his daughter's shoulders.

Krista stands riveted, waiting.

"I think it was... Hilders? Near Oberweid?"

Josef observes Krista, now distraught.

"Why?"

Krista examines the leather seat of the cart. It is stained with what appears to have been blood. She walks around the cart. One side shows the wood stained with blood.

"I think I rode on this cart on the way up here..."

Horst ventured, "With who?"

"Mila."

Horst looks back in shock.

"You COULDN'T have."

Krista glances back. "I DID. Just a few days ago. I took the train to Oberweid and began walking to where we are now. She was with me, the man and the boy."

Krista runs her hands over the stained wood.

Josef exclaimed, "That's impossible."

Horst reaches to stop him. "Josef... not yet."

"THAT'S impossible, Krista. I've had this cart... I used it – to escape."

Krista's eyes ball like saucers in shock.

Horst reaches for Krista.

"No, Papa. We must find out what happened to her. Did she take the train after all?"

Josef explains, "She must have gotten away. Only a man, a prisoner of war, and a young boy was with him. No girl."

Krista dashes to collect her pack.

Horst detains her. "NO, please. Daughter, we will eat. Then, tomorrow, I will show you."

"SHOW me?!"

"Both of you."

"Show me what?"

Horst grapples for words. "Mila. Where she died."

57

WHERE THERE WAS LAUGHTER, there are now tears. The sun rose later than usual as the leaves began falling, heralding the beginning of the autumn season.

Krista places wild mums on Mila's grave, roughly piled up leaves and dirt that Horst had put together in an effort to give the girl some respect. The skeleton still hangs above on a tree, the skull thankfully turned away.

Phoebe has something in her mouth, which she proffers to Horst. Krista sees it immediately, the embroidered handkerchief with the peony flower on it.

She clutches it to her breast.

Then Josef sees his own photograph as a child, next to Mila's notebook.

A shiver runs through him.

Josef pulls the cart like a horse without a halter while Horst pushes from behind. They piled all their belongings into the cart, the dog walking ahead to forage and check for anyone ahead.

Krista walks behind the cart, lost in her thoughts, looking occasionally behind her for anyone who might be following, alive or dead.

EPILOGUE

RUSSIA OCCUPIED the northern areas of Germany and was making their way down south. By the fall of 1945, when the first of the Red Army arrived in Frankfurt and the surrounding little villages, Krista, her father, Horst, and Josef had crossed over to the little village of Teisendorf, northwest of Salzburg, Austria. They brought with them an exhausted Phoebe, who foraged for food on behalf of her masters all the way to Austria.

Krista had travelled almost one hundred miles mostly by foot through forests to find her father. Horst walked for over five months by his own recollection, heading south while Krista headed north. They both subsisted on clover, mushrooms, fish and small game when it was available. When the weather or fear of detection stood in their way, they both stopped for several days and weeks, hiding and foraging.

Mila's ill-fated love for Josef saved his life when he defected from his platoon, disguised as a fruit-seller around the summer of 1944, as he recounted to Krista. He used the horse-drawn cart he found at the train station minutes after his platoon shot and killed both Edgar and Holzer in the ill-fated ride to sell fruit and vegetables with Mila at the station. It was the same platoon that forced Mila into the cattle car, where she escaped hours later, only to plummet seventy-five feet to her death onto the forest floor.

Mila and her hosts Edgar and Holzer were all dead by the time Krista entered the farmstead in the summer of 1945.

Krista and her father emigrated to the United States on a ship that entered the harbor of New York City in 1949.

Horst resumed his trade as a tailor in Philadelphia until his death. Krista eventually met and married a Frenchman.

Krista never saw her mother again. She returned to Frankfurt, Germany, and after several visits discovered and found she had a brother who had escaped imprisonment in Africa. They met for the first time in 1949 shortly before she and her father emigrated to the United States. Brother and sister again visited and gained closure before he passed away in 2019 of old age.

At the time of this writing, Krista still lives in Pennsylvania and has a son, a daughter and a grandson.

She is ninety years old.

PHOTOGRAPHS

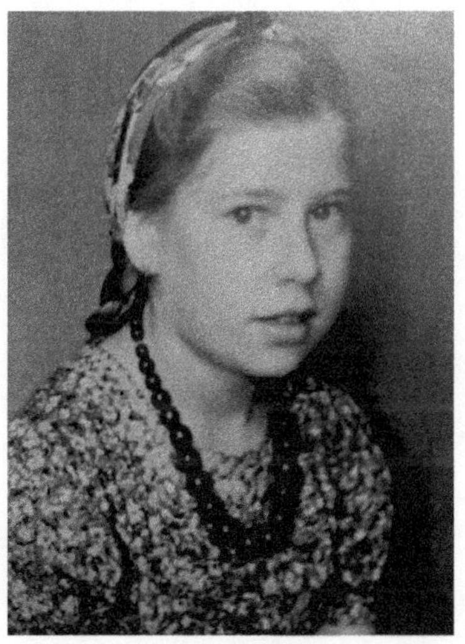

Krista, age 12, he year she was recruited as a Nazi Youth member.

Krista at age eight with cousins and friends. Lower right in braids. Bleichenbach, Germany.

Krista, age 15

Krista, age 16, after the war.

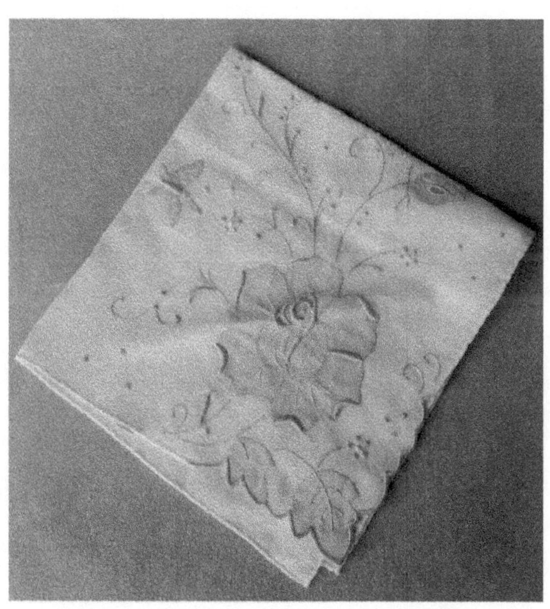

One of Agatha's embroidered handkerchiefs, tagged for sale.

ABOUT THE AUTHOR

Anna Maria Manalo is a practicing therapist and retired school counselor by profession. A former field investigator for MUFON, she placed in several competitions for her supernatural and science fiction screenplays based on real cases:

"The Tulpa Effect", retitled "From Within Me" placed #6 in the top ten in Script Vamp's DreamQuest competition of 2012. The same screenplay was a Quarterfinalist in the 2011 Page International Screenwriting Awards and Third Round Finalist at the AAA Screenwriting Competition. Supernatural thriller "Under Tango Road" placed 'Strongly Consider' at the Creative World Awards for the highly skilled use of subtext and handling of difficult subject matter.

Anna's sci fi screenplay "Uncharted Darkness", placed as a Quarterfinalist at the prestigious Fade-In Awards competition and sci fi thriller "Anomaly" placed as a finalist at The Writers' Place Competition.

Anna has adapted for the screen books by noted UFOlogists Philip Mantle and Paul Stonehill whose working titles are "High Strangeness" and "Height 611".

She has traveled to over 27 countries to date, collecting accounts of alien encounters and hauntings alike which she compiled in her first book, "Portal: A Lifetime of Paranormal Experiences". She has guest starred in over 45 podcasts including Midnight in the Desert, Coast to Coast AM with Connie Willis, Darkness Radio with Dave Schrader, The Paracast, Howard Hughes of UK Radio, Late Night in the Midlands among others. She starred in the second episode of UFO's Over Earth featuring herself as Elisa Simon on the Discovery Channel in 2008.

She lives in Pennsylvania.

ALSO BY ANNA MARIA MANALO

Portal: A Lifetime Of Paranormal Experiences

www.ingramcontent.com/pod-product-compliance
Lightning Source LLC
LaVergne TN
LVHW041315080426
835513LV00008B/463

* 9 7 8 1 9 5 4 5 2 8 1 8 5 *